Pra

The Journey to Ultimate Friendship

"Through story after story, Mike offers something like a tutorial in friendship—both with Jesus and with others. In an age that is increasingly isolated and lonely, such a tutorial is desperately needed. I pray these wonderfully personal stories will arouse a hunger in us all for greater intimacy with God and with one another!"
—Fr. John Riccardo, missionary, Leadership Team, ACTS XXIX

"I count Mike as one of my dearest friends. Through Mike, I have learned to see and approach Jesus as a friend. Yes, Jesus is Lord over all things, but he is also one of us; every bit the almighty God, and every bit a man. In this wonderful and important book, we journey through Mike's life and his friends, particularly that great and most faithful of friends, our Lord Jesus."
—James J. Ackerman, President and Chief Executive Officer, Prison Fellowship

"Michael Timmis has done more than almost any man I know to help people enter into a friendship with Jesus. This book is inspiring!"
—Ralph Martin, STD, President, Renewal Ministries; Director of Graduate Theology Programs in the New Evangelization, Sacred Heart Major Seminary

THE
JOURNEY
TO
ULTIMATE
FRIENDSHIP

Michael T. Timmis

Published by The Word Among Us Press
7115 Guilford Drive, Suite 100
Frederick, Maryland 21704
wau.org

26 25 24 23 22   1 2 3 4 5

ISBN: 978-1-59325-707-1
eISBN: 978-1-59325-708-8

Design by Suzanne Earl

Made and printed in the United States of America

Library of Congress Control Number: 2022918727

To my wife, Nancy—my godly, beautiful wife of sixty years

CONTENTS

Introduction

The experience of authentic friendship has shaped my life in such varied and powerful ways that I almost can't count them. In a very real sense, I am the man I am today because every decision I made emerged from the fruits of friendship. Different friendships have led me on journeys and adventures that I would never have dreamt of as a young man, often taking me to unexpected places in the world and in my spirit.

Throughout this book, I will share these personal stories, breaking open my own history in an attempt to highlight the importance of friendships and to give you some ways to reflect on and apply the wisdom I have gleaned from a lifetime of relationships. In particular, I will share about my friendships with my wife and my son (as a husband and as a father), friendships with prisoners, friendships with the poor, friendships around the world, friendships in tragedy, and friendships with men. I will explore all of these in order to make it crystal clear that there is one fundamental friendship that we all need in our lives: friendship with God in Jesus Christ.

Brothers and sisters, this is the friendship for which the Lord created us. This is the hunger that lies in the depths of our hearts. Despite my own successes in the secular world, for many years it was precisely this friendship that was missing in my life—*even though I was devoutly religious.*

It is my belief that this principle is not being communicated forthrightly or well by my church or many other churches. Ralph Martin, in his book *A Church in Crisis,* quotes the International Theological Commission's document on eschatology:

> In revealing the Father's secrets to us, Jesus wants to make us his friends (cf. John 15:15). But friendship cannot be forced on us. Friendship with God, like adoption, is an offer, to be freely accepted or rejected. . . . This consummated and freely accepted friendship implies a concrete possibility of rejection. What is freely accepted can be freely rejected. [No one who] thus chooses rejection "has any inheritance in the kingdom of Christ and of God" (Ephesians 5:5).[1]

Jesus is a real person who invites us into a friendship that is real and intimate. Yet so many Christians seem to miss this. The problem, I believe, is that very few churches emphasize the humanity of Jesus. As a Catholic, I have always deeply understood and believed in the divinity of Jesus, but it was only when I really began to study the New Testament that I realized how important it is to understand his humanity as well. In many ways, I was an Old Testament Christian. I believed what Deuteronomy 6:4-5 states:

> Hear, O Israel! The LORD is our God, the LORD alone! Therefore, you shall love the LORD, your God, with your whole heart, and with your whole being, and with your whole strength.

Through the grace of God, I never doubted who Jesus was. But it wasn't until I studied the New Testament and saw the words of Jesus in the Great Commandment that I understood his identity more fully.

> Jesus replied, "The first is this: 'Hear, O Israel! The Lord our God is Lord alone! You shall love the Lord your God with all your heart, with all your soul, with all your mind, and with all your strength.' The second is this: 'You shall love your neighbor as yourself.' There is no other commandment greater than these." (Mark 12:29-31)

In the Incarnation, Jesus comes to us as neighbor. God has given us the ability to love and serve him with our minds, because we can now understand him as one of us. And with this grace, we can enter into an eternal friendship with the Father, Son, and Holy Spirit.

As you read this book, I hope that it will help you see how friendships have shaped and changed my life and how they can shape and change yours. My ultimate hope is that you will come to realize that Jesus has invited you into a deep and intimate friendship with him. This is a relationship that can change everything for you, including your eternal destiny.

CHAPTER 1

El Salvador

When I wrote my first book, *Between Two Worlds: The Spiritual Journey of an Evangelical Catholic* (NavPress 2008), I was chairman of the board of Prison Fellowship International, as well as chairman of Prison Fellowship US. In my role with Prison Fellowship International, I visited prisons and met with officials around the world, in an effort to reach out to prisoners in the spirit of Jesus. I carried out the mandate of Jesus: "I was . . . naked and you clothed me, ill and you cared for me, in prison and you visited me" (Matthew 25:35, 36). In my years of going into these prisons, I had many incredible experiences, such as preaching in a Jamaican prison during a riot, visiting death row in Uganda for twenty consecutive years, and visiting a prison in Brazil that was so horrible that the judge who took me there called it "Hell."

A unique prison visit occurred in El Salvador, one of the smallest and most densely populated countries in South America and one very troubled by crime. El Salvador went through a devastating civil war from 1979 to 1992. This was basically a proxy fight between the United States and Russia. The United

States feared that El Salvador might become another Cuba under Russian influence. During the war and afterward, there was terrible violence, perpetrated by military death squads, as well as terrible corruption.

When I went to El Salvador, prison officials told me there were over fifty thousand gang members in the country as a result of the incredible violence the country had endured. Officials took me to a prison where members of MS-13—one of the most violent gangs in the world—made up the entire population. Before I arrived at the prison, the officials set up an elevated stage in a large hall that could accommodate the roughly eight hundred inmates. The hall was divided into two parts, with an aisle down the middle. When I arrived, the men were sitting with their arms folded, looking up at the ceiling. Every single inmate was tattooed with the number thirteen. Many of them were shaved bald, with the number tattooed on their heads as well as on their cheeks and written in cursive on their arms.

The head of the El Salvadoran prison system introduced me as the chairman of Prison Fellowship International, a Christian organization that reaches out to the prisoners of the world. I could see that the inmates could not have cared less about who I was and why I was there. It was obvious that they did not want to be there to hear me but had no choice.

As I looked out over the men, the Holy Spirit compelled me to remove my sport jacket and step down off the stage, much to the consternation of the officials that I was with. I walked slowly to the end of the aisle, dividing the men, not saying a word. Then I turned back and walked to the front, not saying a word. I did that a second time. This took approximately three or four minutes.

Now back at the front, I looked at the men and said, "I have heard about you. You look very tough. I have been in prisons all over the world, and I have met some very tough men, but I have a friend who is the toughest man I ever met. He is tougher than any of you or anyone else. Like some of you, he was beaten and framed. He was unjustly condemned and executed, but he endured all that for me. I do not think any of you would have the courage to die for me or anybody else. So I want to tell you a little bit about him. Some of you know his name, but you don't know anything about him."

While I was speaking, the men sat there with their arms folded, never acknowledging anything I said as they stared off into space. I spoke for about twenty-five minutes about Jesus, about his love for them, about his willingness to forgive them for anything they had done if they only were to ask him for forgiveness. I told them how much Jesus loves each one of them and that he wishes that each one would know who he is and why he came to earth. I continued on, saying that he wanted them to know his love, become his friend, and live eternally with him.

When I finished, there was dead silence. As I stood there in the midst of that silence, the men stirred. All of a sudden, a number of them got up and came to embrace me. I felt deeply moved and saddened for them, for they were sheep without a shepherd, and I knew that I would never see them again. But I thanked God that there would be followers of Jesus who would visit the men, so that what I shared about Jesus might bear fruit.

One of the most difficult aspects of going into a prison is that often you will not have the ability to follow up. In a sense, you are only planting the proverbial seed, and it will be up to others to follow up with those who are touched by the truth of Jesus.

What Mother Teresa said gives me great comfort: that we are called to be faithful, not to achieve results. However, that day proved to me, as I have seen many times since, that the only way to evangelize is to use words that people understand, words like "friend." That is the reason I have written this book: to help people understand that the only way we can fully embrace Jesus is through relationship. Friendship is an experience that everyone understands, so if we speak to others about Jesus as friend, we have the greatest opportunity to help them see the richness of life in Christ, which Jesus is inviting them to receive.

Personal Application

Take a few moments, either by yourself or in a small group, and reflect on the following questions. You can share your answers with others when you have finished your reflection.

1. Have you ever been in a tense situation or a situation in which you didn't know what to say? What happened, and how did you find the solution or the words? Was Jesus involved in that solution? Why or why not?

2. Was it shocking or unusual in any way to hear Jesus described as a friend who was tougher than any gang member present? How, or why not?

3. If someone asked you to describe what Jesus was like, how would you describe him?

CHAPTER 2

My Early Years

In my autobiography, *Between Two Worlds*, I went into detail about my background, leading up to the encounter with Jesus that changed my life. Here, in order for the reader to understand the premise of this book, it is necessary to provide sufficient understanding of the history of my life.

The youngest of five children, I grew up on the west side of Detroit, in a devout Irish Catholic family. My parents were in their midforties when I was born, so I never knew them the way my brothers and sisters did. My mother was never in good health, as she had congestive heart failure, and my father, who worked very hard, was a quiet, reserved man. We were a very religious family; we prayed as a family and went to church regularly.

We lived in a densely populated Irish neighborhood, a wonderful area in which to grow up. We never locked our front door; I'm not even sure we had a key. I could go out and play and move around without any threat of danger. The houses were very small, so kids played outdoors all the time and would only come home for dinner or to do their homework. It was a very strict neighborhood in the sense that everybody knew everybody else's business.

One day on the playground near my school, I said a swear word. I must have been about eleven. When I walked in the door of our home, my mother slapped my face and told me to never say that word again. Apparently, a mother who lived near the school had heard me yell the word and immediately called my mother. That is an example of how tight our neighborhood was.

My life changed dramatically when, in seventh grade, I went on a Boy Scout weekend. It rained for three days and was extremely windy. Our tent blew down, so I was wet and cold for three days. By the time we headed back home on the bus, I felt very sick. I had asked the scoutmaster to call my parents, but he refused, telling me to "man up."

By the time we got home, I could not walk off the bus. I immediately went to the hospital, where I was eventually diagnosed with rheumatic fever and pneumonia. This changed my life dramatically, as I suddenly became bedridden. I missed the rest of seventh grade as well as half of eighth grade, when I had a recurrence of rheumatic fever. My parents were very concerned. They thought I was going to die.

As a result of my sickness, I developed a heart murmur. When I went to high school, which is now called University of Detroit Jesuit High School, I could only climb the stairs once a day. Freshmen classes were on the third floor, so I had to take my lunch and a book up with me and eat by myself. I never had an opportunity to be with my classmates in the cafeteria.

This caused me to have low self-esteem. I also put on a lot of weight, as I could not do anything physical.

Early Grief

My mother died suddenly on Easter night, April 11, 1955, during my sophomore year of high school. I was devastated! The night she died, I could hear my brother Jerry, who was a senior in medical school, and my brother Hilary, a junior, shouting to her doctor on the phone that they had given my mother a shot of adrenalin, but it was not working. I walked into my mother's bedroom and asked her what was wrong. She could not speak but pulled her hand up from under the pillow and held up the crucifix on her rosary and then died. I experienced the pain of losing not only my mother but also my best friend.

Within a year and a half, each of my sisters had married, and my brothers had left to do residency in their specialties—Jerry as a cardiologist and Hilary as a heart surgeon. I was extremely lonely because my physical limitations didn't allow me to interact with friends. My father was overwhelmed with grief, and in all that time, we never had a substantive conversation.

Between my junior and senior years in high school, I determined to make a change in my life. During the summer, I fasted and lost over thirty pounds. Simultaneously, I grew four or five inches. So when I went back to school for my senior year, my classmates could hardly recognize me.

A Friend Indeed

During that year, God sent me a friend who would have a tremendous influence on the course of my life. His name was Mike Sullivan. Mike was an all-state swimmer and probably the most popular guy in school. He not only befriended me, but he also became like a brother. I spent a tremendous amount of time at his house. He was part of a big Irish family, and his parents were very easygoing, allowing me to stay many nights in their home.

A tremendous example of Mike's friendship occurred when we were in college. Five of us drove up north to go skiing and to stay at Mike's parents' cottage, which was on a lake near Gaylord, Michigan. It was snowing very heavily on our drive up. When we arrived at the road that led off the main highway to the cottage, we got stuck in a snowdrift. We decided to walk to the cottage.

Because the cottage was two to three miles off the main highway, we opted not to take our luggage. None of us were dressed for the cold, and the snow was deep. When we were about a mile away, one of our friends, Andy, said he could not walk any farther. He lay down in the snow, wanting to sleep. We knew this was extremely serious, so we took turns pulling him across the snow until we finally reached the cottage.

When we got inside, we saw that there was no wood for the fireplace; someone had used all of it. There was no way to heat the house. It was very cold, and we sat in a circle with blankets around us. We were deeply worried about our friend, who had promptly fallen asleep.

In the middle of the night, Mike asked me if I had taken my penicillin that day, and I told him that I had left it in the car. (I had suffered rheumatic fever twice, so I took penicillin pills, and later shots, until I was thirty-five years old.) Suddenly Mike disappeared, and he was gone for about an hour and a half. He walked through the snow to the car, retrieved my bag with the penicillin, and walked back to give it to me.

When morning came, Mike left again. He walked out to the road for help and somehow got the Gaylord Rescue Service to come on snowmobiles and take us all out. Now whenever I read John 15:13, "No one has greater love than this, to lay down one's life for one's friends," I am reminded of Mike and the fact that he walked over twelve miles in deep snow to save us. What an example of a heroic friend!

As an aside, I kept in contact with Mike over the years, even though he lived in a different state. For many years, my wife, Nancy, and I, along with others, put on a weekend retreat to share Jesus with our friends. One year I invited Mike Sullivan and his wife, Diane, to come to the retreat. At the end of the retreat, he said, "I know this is great for you, but it's not for me." I replied that I understood, and it did not affect our friendship.

Years later I got a call from Mike Sullivan. He was living in Dallas, Texas. He said, "I've read your book and have asked Jesus into my life. Could I come and see you?" He and Diane did come, and as we talked, Mike asked me to mentor him. He suggested that we have a call every week or ten days, and I could teach him something about Jesus.

Mike died suddenly three years later; he is now with Jesus. I thank God for this dear man who helped me when I badly needed a friend.

Personal Application

Take a few moments, either by yourself or in a small group, and reflect on the following questions. You can share your answers with others when you have finished your reflection.

1. Have you ever had a friend do something exceptional to help you out of a jam or a dangerous situation? What did you think about your friend after their assistance?

2. Have you ever helped a friend out of a difficult or dangerous situation? What was it like for you? How did you feel about your friend afterward?

3. What do you think Jesus' thoughts about you were when he hung on the cross to ransom you from sin and death?

4. Is it difficult for you to think of Jesus as a friend giving his life for you? Why or why not?

CHAPTER 3

Meeting Nancy

When I was a freshman in college, I came home from school one day to find the woman who lived across the street, a widow with a young son, hanging out in our house with my father. Before I could wrap my mind around what was happening, my father said to me, "Meet your new mother."

I was shocked. My dad had not told me that he was getting married! Though I knew he had been visiting this neighbor for many months, he had not once talked to me about her. This news devastated me.

I retreated even further from my home, spending most of my time with the many friends I had now made. Those friendly relationships kept me from being rebellious or bitter.

I had started college at the University of Detroit, then transferred to Wayne State University, which was less expensive. My father had pressured me from my youth to become a doctor, like my brothers, and Wayne State had a good medical school. I was working my way through college and had very little money. I would often go to a cafeteria with friends, and

I would simply mix hot water with ketchup to make "tomato soup," rounding the meal out with the free crackers on the table.

In my junior year, I observed this girl going through the line at the cafeteria each day. She fascinated me; there was something about her demeanor that was totally different from that of any other girl I knew. So I found a way to meet her and discovered that her name was Nancy Lauppe. She was dating a young man at the University of Michigan, but I decided to press her for a date. She went out with me, and I fell hopelessly in love. Over the next year and a half, we broke up three times but always got back together. I asked her to marry me on Christmas Eve, 1961.

Nancy's father was a doctor who specialized in eye, ear, nose, and throat surgery. While he was very reserved, Nancy's mother was very outgoing. They were a wonderful balance of personalities, which helped them have a successful marriage.

When I asked Dr. Lauppe for permission to marry his only daughter, he assumed we would marry in the Episcopal Church, which as a Catholic I could not do. The next few months were very tense, but ultimately, I arranged for us to get married at St. Mary's in Toledo, Ohio, thanks to my parish priest. We married upon graduation, and I have to say that Nancy was very brave. Not only did she have to sign documents affirming that we would raise our children Catholic, but we were also married in a breezeway to the church, and the gardener and his wife were our witnesses!

Five days later, a judge married us again in the living room of her family's home. It was a very quiet experience, and we had no reception. At that time, Nancy's father would only refer to me as Mr. Timmis, which was embarrassing. However, because Nancy had sacrificed so much, I didn't let it bother me.

Nancy's dad continued to refer to me as Mr. Timmis until I graduated at the top of my law school class, Nancy and I bought a house, and I secured a job with the law firm of my choice. My father-in-law, Fred, was impressed with what I had accomplished. Over the years we became extremely close friends; in fact, he was like a father to me. When I could not talk to my own father, I could always reach out to my father-in-law—and we had tremendous discussions. Each Sunday our family would go to my in-laws' house for dinner.

In the winter of 1971, nine years into our marriage, Nancy's father was scheduled to have a catheterization on a Monday. Even so, we made it to Sunday dinner. After the evening had ended, we bundled our two children into their snowsuits and said our goodbyes. We were all in the car when Nancy's dad came out of the house and asked us to come back inside. Nancy and I were quite surprised.

Nancy's dad took me aside and told me he had a premonition of death. I said to him, "Dad, you are only sixty-five, and this is a routine catheterization, which should go very well."

He said, "If anything happens to me, you are the head of the family. I have made you the executor of my estate, and I want you to take care of the family." He also said, "Before you go, I would like to drink a toast to the family."

Nancy's dad went to the basement and brought up a bottle of warm champagne that someone had given him years before. We opened it, had a drink, and toasted the family. When we got back into the car, I said to Nancy, "Your father is very sentimental."

The next day, I was in a meeting when a call came from Nancy. She told me to rush to Harper Hospital. By the time I arrived, her father had died of an embolism caused by the procedure.

Nancy's father was not only my father-in-law but also one of my best friends. Losing another friend like him greatly saddened me. In fact, I grieved for many years.

Personal Application

Take a few moments, either by yourself or in a small group, and reflect on the following questions. You can share your answers with others when you have finished your reflection.

1. Not every friendship starts out perfectly. Have you ever met someone with whom you didn't get along or seemingly had nothing in common but who later became a good friend? What happened to change that relationship? How has that relationship enriched your life?

2. Life can change in an instant, and we can lose those close to us. Have you ever lost a friend unexpectedly? What happened, and how did you cope with that loss?

3. Sometimes friends have a falling-out from which they never recover. Have you ever had a friendship end suddenly? Did you try to repair the relationship? What was the result, and how has that result affected your life?

4. Imagine you made a friend who would be with you throughout your entire life, someone who would never leave you because of an argument or be taken from you by illness, someone you could always talk to and count on. What would that friendship be worth to you? How might that friend affect your life?

CHAPTER 4

Practicing Law

Upon graduation from law school, I joined an entrepreneurial law firm. The partners indicated to me that I would receive a small percentage of any company the firm bought. That inspired me to think like an entrepreneur and work very hard.

The law firm was very strict. We usually worked at least sixty-hour weeks, Monday through Friday, and at least half a day on Saturday. The firm had a formal culture and did not tolerate mistakes. True to my nature, I worked incredibly hard (becoming a workaholic, truth be told), and within five years, I was made a partner.

I loved the practice of law in those days. We worked on a lot of mergers and acquisitions and represented some very large as well as middle-sized companies. By the time I made partner, I had become the chief "rainmaker" in the firm, somewhat to the consternation of the older partners. This became evident in 1975, when the president of our largest client, a public corporation, insisted that I go to Japan to determine why over a million dollars was missing from the company's Japanese subsidiary.

I didn't work on that client's legal business. However, the president thought I was much tougher than any of the other partners. He hoped I would get to the bottom of the problem, which the team of executives sent over previously had failed to figure out. I had never been abroad. When all of this happened, I was in California working for another client and had come down with a very bad cold.

Before I left for Japan, the president made it clear that I had the power to hire and fire in accord with my judgment. When I arrived in Tokyo, everyone there was fearful that they would be fired, and consequently, they were very obsequious toward me. I went through the books and could see that money was missing, but I did not understand why. I made the decision to fire the company's lawyers because they were of no help, and I hired a new firm to help me interrogate every member of the firm.

During one of these interrogations, I could tell that a female secretary was lying to me. After an extensive examination, she told me that her boyfriend, whom she called Mr. X, was part of a plot to defraud the company. She negotiated with me and said that if I chose not to prosecute Mr. X, he would tell me the whole story. I just had to meet him at 2:00 a.m. at a certain hotel. As I look back, this was a crazy and dangerous thing to do because of the amount of money involved.

I met the man, and he revealed that the local head of our company had conspired with one of the largest Japanese construction companies to falsify bills and extort a huge amount of money from the parent company. Everything began to make sense. So I contacted the president back in Detroit and told him that I had figured out the problem. He decided to convene a board of directors meeting the next day, and I was to call and explain everything. This was serious, as we were a publicly traded company and had to notify the US Securities and Exchange Commission of any embezzlement or bribes.

With the time difference, I had to call the company at 2:00 a.m., Tokyo time. With all the travel, stress, and odd hours, my cold had developed into something more. I now had a high fever, and my voice was disappearing. In the middle of my explanation to the board, I lost my voice completely. I couldn't say a word; there was just silence from my end of the phone.

I could hear the board members getting really worried. Some of them said, "They killed him! They got to him!" It was frustrating because I could hear them but couldn't communicate (we didn't have emails or texting in those days). So I hung up and lay down on the bed.

At 6:00 a.m. and just barely able to speak, I called a partner at Arthur Anderson who was in Tokyo. He was the only friend that I knew I could trust. He took me to the hospital, where the doctors confirmed that I had pneumonia. I was quickly hospitalized.

I have worn a medal of Mary since I married Nancy, to remind me of fidelity to my wife. As the hospital staff were taking an x-ray, a Japanese nurse asked me if I was "katrick" (Catholic), but I couldn't understand her. So she grabbed my medal and asked again, indicating that she was also Catholic. This time I understood perfectly.

This experience gave me a tremendous sense of peace. I have had a deep friendship with Mother Mary all my life. In that moment, I knew she was praying for me. Further, it was an affirmation that Jesus was protecting me. In future years of travel from country to country witnessing to Jesus, I always remembered how Jesus had assured me that he was always with me.

Personal Application

Take a few moments, either by yourself or in a small group, and reflect on the following questions. You can share your answers with others when you have finished your reflection.

1. Do you have friends whom you can call on for assistance even if you are in another country? Have you ever needed to do that? What happened?

2. Have you ever met a fellow believer during a difficult or stressful experience? How did that connection change your experience of the situation?

3. Have you considered the role of Mary and the saints who have gone before us in heaven? What if they are our closest Christian friends, whom we can call on at any time for prayers?

4. How might Mary and the saints remind us of the love Jesus has for us?

CHAPTER 5

Two New Friends

When I was made a partner in my law firm at age thirty, I felt tremendously blessed. I had everything I wanted: a loving wife, two children, and a career. I also had met two people who would become close friends. God would use both of them to shape the course of my life.

One was an African American woman named Marie, who was a widow with five children. Nancy and I decided that we were very blessed and that it was time to share our blessings with someone else. We decided the best way to do this was to work with a poor family in the inner city. Through contact with a priest friend, I learned about a widow who had just lost both her husband and one of her children.

I was embarrassed and nervous when I called Marie to explain who I was and how I had reached her. Her response was "So you want to become a limousine liberal?"

I replied, "I don't have a limousine, and I am not liberal."

She said, "What I really need now is a friend. If you are offering friendship, I accept."

That friendship lasted for many, many years, and it taught me much about the struggles of life in the inner city. Marie was a hero. She lived for her children, and she was an example of deep faith in Jesus in the midst of adversity.

As I look back on my friendship with Marie, I realize that it was the beginning of a lifelong caring for others that took Nancy and me in many different directions. We started in the inner city of Detroit and eventually went to many places around the world. I believe this was prompted by our deep faith in the Catholic tradition of helping others.

The other friend was a man named Randy Agley, a business partner who became like a brother to me. Our relationship was the catalyst of a significant change in my work life, moving me from being a lawyer to being a businessman. This change was significant.

When I met Randy, he was an accountant at Arthur Andersen, which in the 1970s was the number one accounting firm in the world. Our respective firms had many mutual clients, and thus we began to work together and soon became friends. One day I was able to do a personal favor for him, and he repaid me by sending many clients to our firm. Through this we grew closer and closer, establishing mutual admiration and trust.

Randy sent me one client who wanted to sell a landfill to a company in Houston, Texas. The client wanted a quarter of a million dollars. Fifty years ago, that was a lot of money. I went with him to Houston and there negotiated a deal that resulted in his receiving almost two million dollars. On the flight back, we shared with each other how much we knew about buying businesses. We concluded that we could do the same for ourselves, if only we had the money.

Soon that thought became a reality. Some of Randy's clients at Arthur Andersen were the largest McDonald's franchisees in the country. They decided to sell their interests back to McDonald's, which resulted in a huge return. They wanted to start an investment company with Randy, and Randy invited me to be his partner. This enabled us to start buying companies.

Standing for Jesus

Randy and I remained partners for thirty-six years. We purchased many companies, from Boston to Los Angeles and in Europe, as well as many real estate projects. We employed thousands of people. Randy is one of the brightest men I have ever met, with a computer-like mind, able to comprehensively analyze any deal. We had a symbiotic relationship that worked even though we had very different personalities. The truth is that our business relationship was grounded in our personal friendship, and that made it exceptionally strong.

Randy observed the dramatic change in me after I gave my life totally to Jesus. One day he told me that I never had to worry about losing my temper again because even though he knew I had really changed, not everyone would believe that. We had a great laugh. That kind of banter was characteristic of our friendship throughout the years.

One important incident in our relationship occurred during a meeting with the president of our development company. We owned a strip mall in Lansing, Michigan, that was losing a tremendous amount of money. This was back in the day when large companies like Blockbuster made a business out of renting movies. Another company had approached us, wanting to lease a significant amount of square footage for such an operation. When I found out that this company rented X-rated movies, I told the president of our development company that we would not enter into the lease.

One day in a meeting, Randy pointed out how much money we were losing in this center, and the president snidely remarked, "Well, you know your partner; he will not let us enter into a lease." When my partner asked me why, I pointed out to him that they rented X-rated movies. Without missing a beat, Randy said, "If that is Mike's decision, then that is what we live with." I loved the fact that he backed me up without hesitation.

God honored our partnership. The success that Randy and I achieved in purchasing companies enabled us to create significant wealth. This eventually allowed Nancy and me the independence to travel throughout the world to evangelize and visit prisoners on every continent, as well as to fund projects for the poor in Peru, Honduras, Nicaragua, and throughout East Africa. All this work proceeded through the friendships we made and with the ultimate aim of introducing Jesus to the people we were trying to help.

Personal Application

Take a few moments, either by yourself or in a small group, and reflect on the following questions. You can share your answers with others when you have finished your reflection.

1. People are more than just objects of our charity and care; they are manifestations of the love and creative goodness of God. If we remain open, those whom we serve can be instruments of God's grace, changing our lives. Have you ever encountered someone who needed your help but who also touched or changed your life in significant ways? What happened?

2. Looking at the Gospels, what were Jesus' interactions like with those who were poor, downtrodden, and outcast? What do Jesus' words and actions say about our own attitudes, actions, and obligations to those who are suffering? How do we live out these obligations in our daily lives?

3. Have you ever had to take a costly stand based on your Christian beliefs? What was the situation, and how did you respond? How would the presence and support of a friend have influenced, assisted, or changed your response?

4. Can you name a time when you had the opportunity to support a friend when he or she took a stand on their Christian belief? How did you respond?

CHAPTER 6

My Friendship
with Doug Coe

After Randy and I started buying companies, it seemed as if I was hardly ever home. I worked a great deal and traveled frequently, particularly to California, where we had many business interests. When I was home, I was tired and tense, and I did not communicate with Nancy, the only woman I have ever loved. Our only discussions revolved around the children.

I began to feel dead inside. I was retreating from Nancy and retreating from the Lord. I would go to Mass each Sunday, receive Communion, and pray to God that I could feel something. I had no one with whom to talk to about this, and I had no idea what to do.

One night during this nadir of our marriage, Nancy persuaded me to go to a dinner with her. There, for the first time in my life, I heard a businessman get up and talk about his friendship with Jesus. His words helped me realize that, while I was very devout, I did not have a personal friendship with

Jesus. That night I turned everything in my life over to him and committed myself to following him.

At first Nancy and I did not talk about the evening. Two weeks later, she told me that she had likewise committed all her life to Jesus. Shortly thereafter I was invited to a Bible study, which I went to reluctantly but which proved quite interesting. I quickly became friends with the man who was leading the study, Dick Robarts. This friendship shaped me in a new way. Dick taught me about Scripture for many hours each week.

One day Dick asked me to go to Washington to meet a man named Doug Coe, who was the architect of the National Prayer Breakfast and leader of the House and Senate prayer groups. My resulting friendship with Doug became incredibly impactful. He began to mentor me and teach me about friendship with Jesus.

Doug Coe was one of the most amazing men I had ever met. He had a God-given anointing to lead people to Jesus. He had a compassion and empathy that allowed him to create instant friendships with those with whom he was meeting—whatever their background, nationality, or religion. The stories of his meetings with leaders around the world are legendary. At a National Prayer Breakfast, President H. W. Bush called Doug one of America's greatest ambassadors. Doug desired to bring reconciliation through Jesus to every country in the world— particularly to places that no one would think reachable, like North Korea, Iran, and Afghanistan.

Throughout our years of friendship, Doug and I talked constantly about Jesus and about expanding the kingdom. Traveling with him was like living the Book of Acts. Doug was particularly anxious to establish small prayer groups in which men and women could learn to live a life like Jesus' and thus become reconcilers. He exemplified to me more than any other person the words from Second Corinthians: "God was reconciling the world to himself in Christ, not counting their trespasses against them and entrusting to us the message of reconciliation. So we are ambassadors for Christ, as if God were appealing through us" (5:19-20).

That last sentence, "So we are ambassadors for Christ, as if God were appealing through us," has impacted me as much as any line in Scripture. I realize that wherever I go, I represent Jesus, who is in me. It is his presence within me that gives me the great honor and responsibility of representing friendship with him to others.

Personal Application

Take a few moments, either by yourself or in a small group, and reflect on the following questions. You can share your answers with others when you have finished your reflection.

1. Friendship with Jesus is both like and unlike other friendships in our lives. All loving relationships are ultimately acts of the will, because love is an action of the will. Can you recall a time in your life when you definitively decided that you would commit yourself to another person as their friend? What happened after you made that decision?

2. One can only have a personal relationship with a real person, and real persons have characteristics and personalities. Thinking about the Person of Jesus, can you name some of his characteristics? How would you describe his personality to others?

3. Looking at your relationship with Jesus, would you characterize it as an intentional, personal friendship with him? If yes, in what ways do you live out your commitment to Jesus Christ as friend and Savior? If no, what do you think are the reasons for this? What would need to change for you to commit yourself totally to friendship with Jesus?

CHAPTER 7

Meeting with
Special Friends

Almost immediately after I committed everything in my
life to Jesus, I started meeting with friends for the purpose of sharing the joy I had found in him. I went to two of
my closest friends at that time and asked if they would like to
study the Bible with me. They both said no. So I countered with
this proposition: "We all have teenagers," I said. "How about
getting together and praying for our families?" They agreed.

We started meeting together on Wednesday evenings, and in
a few short months, the group grew to approximately twenty
men. We met together for twenty-five years, and we did study
Scripture. Both of the wonderful men who prompted me to
start those gatherings are now in heaven.

Shortly after beginning those Wednesday sessions, I was
asked to speak to a group of young Evangelical businessmen.
The day after my talk, one of the men came to my office to see
me. He said that although he had graduated from a seminary,
he had never heard anyone talk about Jesus in the way I did.

He wanted me to teach him. He said he would like a lifelong friendship with me, with Jesus as the center of the relationship. He also asked if he could have an office in our building. Needless to say, I was overwhelmed. I told him that making these decisions would take a great deal of prayer on my part. He would have to meet with my wife and my son, who was in Africa at that time, because I considered this a very serious request. He agreed to that.

We formed a covenant as friends and brothers in Jesus. He is responsible for bringing reconciliation to the Democrats and Republicans in the Michigan legislature and in the US Congress, as well as many other aspects of reconciliation. Chuck McLeod and I continue our covenant of friendship and brotherhood to this day.

In addition to my newfound friendship with Chuck, the other Evangelical businessmen to whom I spoke asked me to start a Bible study for them. We met every Thursday morning, and while some men came and went according to the seasons of their lives, the group continued for thirty-one years. I developed tremendous friendships with many of the men, including one named Ed Russell. In addition, many from that group started their own meetings, which continue to this day.

After selling the last of my business interests, I approached Ed Russell, who owns numerous rental properties in Grosse Pointe, Michigan, in an area I called "The Hill." I asked Ed if he could find office space for my secretary and the person who oversees our foundation investments. He said that he would like me to move into his office space. He would rearrange his offices to accommodate me. He had one condition: that we would meet an hour a week to discuss our relationship with Jesus, our families, and our everyday lives.

Needless to say, I was delighted. For the past fifteen years, every Tuesday from 9:00 to 10:00 a.m., Ed and I have met either in person or on Zoom. Ed has become closer to me than even my own brothers. He is a tremendous example of someone who shares friendship with Jesus and one of the most approachable men I have ever met. People of all backgrounds recognize that he is special and want to be friends with him.

In addition to the two friendships I just mentioned, there are a number of men with whom I have been meeting for years on a somewhat unscheduled basis. Despite the irregular sessions, each time we gather, I am moved by the goodness of God at work in the lives of these men and am touched deeply by his goodness to me. The wonderful technology of video conferencing has enabled me to stay in touch with friends all over the United States and in Africa, Europe, and Latin America. This contact keeps our friendships current and significant.

Over thirty years ago, Doug Coe and I started meeting with a small group of Christian leaders, to grow deeper in our knowledge and experience of Jesus. For the past twenty-two years, I have hosted an annual meeting of that group in our home in Naples. Twelve men from around the country come, and we spend almost three days deepening our friendship with Jesus and each other through prayer, fellowship, and quiet reflection. Our sole purpose is to be together. There are no agendas or requests made of each other, just a mutual sharing of the love of Jesus that each of us has. Meeting with friends in this way results in personal growth in holiness and passion for the work of God.

Personal Application

Take a few moments, either by yourself or in a small group, and reflect on the following questions. You can share your answers with others when you have finished your reflection.

1. Have you ever met regularly with friends to support one another, either personally or in a professional capacity? If so, what was that like? If not, have you ever given thought as to what you might want out of such meetings?

2. Have you met regularly with friends to focus on your relationship with Jesus? How have those meetings impacted your life?

3. Friendship with Jesus includes friendships with others who believe in him. These relationships enable us to grow in love of God and neighbor. Identify three friends whom you think you would like to connect with regularly, and invite them to join you for prayer and discussion about Jesus and about life. The structure doesn't have to be formal—although sometimes that does help groups continue longer. It can be as simple as gathering over a meal to pray, catch up, and talk about Jesus with each other.

CHAPTER 8

The Touch of Jesus

One of the things I found in my travels is that after I spoke, particularly when there was a small group of men, they wanted to embrace as a sign of friendship. I believe it was the joy of Jesus that filled us through his grace.

When I started studying Scripture, I realized how many times Jesus reached out and physically touched people, reflecting his love and friendship with them. As he moved through crowds, hundreds of people must have wanted to touch him, especially because so many were healed when they touched him (or even his clothes). I had a glimpse of what it must have been like for Jesus when I and a small group of friends visited Mother Teresa in Calcutta in 1989.

Mother Teresa did not have an office. If you wanted to be with her, you had to walk with her while she worked. She had many little houses in the middle of Calcutta that held babies and the terminally ill. As we walked from one place to another, hundreds of people, mostly Hindu, touched her toes. It was amazing to me that she did not stumble, because the streets of Calcutta were the most crowded streets I have ever seen. She seemed oblivious to all the people touching her feet. I remember thinking that this must have been what Jesus experienced as he moved about.

In Scripture we read of many people whom Jesus touched: a man with leprosy (see Matthew 8:2-3), a twelve-year-old girl in Capernaum (Mark 5:41-42), the blind man just outside of Bethsaida (8:22-25), the servant of the high priest whose ear Peter had cut off in the Garden of Gethsemane (Luke 22:50-51), and numerous others. As my faith deepened, I began to understand the touch of Jesus.

I was in Buenos Aires visiting friends. A great friend of mine, Bill Murchison, who was a regular visitor to prisons, asked me to accompany him to a large prison in the city at night (which I normally did not do, for obvious reasons). I remember going into this decrepit place, where there were holes in the stairs as we climbed up to a meeting room. (Thank God, since I was there, that prison has been closed.) My friend had filled his pockets with toothbrushes, toothpaste, combs, soap, and other items. The room held about two hundred men, and Bill told them, "I have a friend here whom I want you to listen to."

It was over ninety degrees. These poor men were hot, sweating, and only wearing their underwear briefs. As I started to speak, I realized how ridiculous it was. I felt as if I were having an out-of-body experience, and God was laughing at me. I could see myself turning in a circle so that I could engage with my eyes as many men as possible.

As my friend translated, I gave the men my testimony about Jesus. At the end of my talk, the men wanted to embrace me as a sign of friendship and acceptance. I thought to myself, nobody would ever believe this. Here are these men who just heard about Jesus and his unconditional love for them, standing in their underwear, needing to make some physical contact. Despite the strange conditions, it gave me great joy to be there with them.

Another amusing experience occurred in Jinja, Uganda, where my wife and I had gone to a women's prison to speak to the inmates. The matron in charge of the prison was a very large woman dressed in an army uniform because in Uganda the prison officials are in the military. This woman was unhappy I was there, speaking to her charges, and she stood glaring in the corner while I spoke.

However, we returned the following year to speak in the same prison, and the matron was expecting me. As we walked up the sidewalk, she came out, grabbed me, picked me up (she was very large), and twirled me around. She said, "I am so glad you are back." She told me that after listening to me the previous year, she thought about what I had said and then gave her life to Jesus.

I have had a number of experiences speaking to Muslims in the Middle East. Interestingly, after listening to me talk about Jesus, they always want to embrace. In Turkey my mentor Doug Coe and I were invited to meet with the cabinet of the country. Through the mediation of a senator, Doug had met some of these men before. After we were served dinner, they excused the waiters, closed the door, and told us to take them as deep as we could and tell them everything we knew about Jesus.

We met until about 2:00 or 3:00 a.m.; it was amazing. At the end of the meeting, we stood up and asked the men if we could put our arms around each other. Doug then asked me to pray in the name of Jesus. It was one of the most beautiful experiences of my life, as these Muslim men joined with us in friendship in a prayer to Jesus.

As I reflect on this and many other meetings, I know they had nothing to do with me and everything to do with Jesus. I was his stand-in, reaching out in friendship so that he could touch them through his love for me.

Personal Application

Take a few moments, either by yourself or in a small group, and reflect on the following questions. You can share your answers with others when you have finished your reflection.

1. In what ways do you express love to your friends? How do you let them know you love them? How do they express their love to you?

2. Can you imagine a situation in which you and a group of friends or family members experience something extraordinary? For example, what if one of you discovered that they had won the lottery? What would you all do upon hearing the news?

3. Have you ever experienced the joy of Jesus? How would you describe that joy to others? If you have never experienced that kind of joy, what would you hope it to be like?

CHAPTER 9

Friendship Is a Two-Way Street

One of the greatest difficulties men have is receiving. Many men, like myself, love to give, but we do not like to receive. It's especially difficult for us to receive criticism!

True friendship is a two-way street. We must be willing to accept not only the positive, encouraging things our friends say to us but also the challenging, critical things they say in the context of their love for us. The reality is that one of the hardest parts of friendship is to accept the criticism of another friend.

Forty years ago, a dear Jewish friend of mine, Eugene Driker, who is an outstanding lawyer, sent me a five-page handwritten letter telling me I was working too hard, not sleeping enough, drinking too much, and too hard on myself and others. If I did not wake up, Eugene warned, my success would be meaningless because my family would be destroyed.

This was a very hard letter to receive. It began an awakening in me as I realized how empty I was becoming. I would go to Communion each Sunday and pray that I could feel something.

While I never doubted that Jesus was my Savior, I felt myself retreating from God, and it frightened me.

Shortly thereafter, at the outreach dinner I wrote about in chapter 6, I had an encounter with Jesus. At that moment, I dedicated every aspect of my life—my marriage, my children, my friends, my family, my career, my wealth—to serving Jesus. That change in my life started the greatest journey I have ever been on, as I move toward the finish line to meet Jesus.

I received criticism once from Doug Coe, who had just spent the weekend at my house. As I drove him back to the airport, he turned to me and said, "I want to tell you something, and I do not want you to say a word until we get to the airport." He then proceeded to inform me that I was insensitive to my wife. Quite frankly, this infuriated me because I felt he was much less sensitive to his wife than I was to mine.

I was quietly and deeply upset, but I did not say a word. I dropped Doug off at the airport, and on my drive home, I started to pray and compare myself to him. I then heard that still, small voice say to me, "I know that not all of it is true, but I believe some of it is true; can you accept that?"

I prayed about it, and the next morning I called Doug and said thank you for pointing the issue out to me. I promised him that I would try to do better. The fact that I did not argue with him or criticize him for the same thing deepened our friendship, love, and trust tremendously.

I believe one of the hallmarks of a true friendship is the ability to accept criticism from a friend. Another hallmark is the willingness to risk the friendship of another by telling him or her the truth in a Christ-centered way.

A friend once told me that his close friend was impeding the work they were doing to promote the gospel. I asked him if he had told his friend what he had just told me, and my friend said he had not because it might terminate their friendship. "Do you not love him enough to tell him the truth?" I asked.

He replied, "I guess I do not."

Needless to say, I was deeply disappointed.

In another instance, I went to a Christian leader who I felt was doing something wrong. I took another brother with me; he was equally close to that man. I explained to the leader what I thought he was doing wrong. He took great offense at my criticizing him. At this point in his ministry, he felt he was beyond being criticized. My friend and I both agreed that what I told this leader was true. It took a very long time for my friendship with this Christian leader to heal.

However, I truly believe that if you care about someone enough, you must tell them the truth, no matter the cost. Jesus modeled true friendship and love his whole life, and this is what he did for those whom he encountered. He revealed truth to his disciples in order to save, protect, heal, deliver, and liberate them. (See, for example, Matthew 16:22-23; Mark 8:31-33; 9:33-37.)

Personal Application

Take a few moments, either by yourself or in a small group, and reflect on the following questions. You can share your answers with others when you have finished your reflection.

1. How well do you accept criticism from your friends? Is it easy or hard for you to act on that criticism?

2. Have you ever had to deliver criticism to a friend? How did the conversation go? What made you hesitant to share your heart with your friend?

3. How do you think Jesus wants to talk to you when addressing those parts of your life that need to be transformed, healed, and changed?

CHAPTER 10

Friends in Tragedy

Almost two years to the day after I committed everything in my life to Jesus, tragedy struck with the death of our daughter. As any parent reading this can imagine, her death has been an integral part of my life.

Laura died at age fifteen. We do not know if she intended to harm herself, but one night she became very upset because we had caught her skipping school and smoking. She knew that we would have to visit her school the next day.

When I woke up the next morning, at 6:30 a.m., I heard Nancy's car running in the garage. I found Laura in the car with the garage door shut. Exhaust fumes filled the car, and I could see Laura lying there unconscious, while the radio played. She was rushed to the hospital. After about an hour, the doctors told us that she was dead.

The first words in my mind came from 1 Corinthians: "No trial has come to you but what is human. God is faithful and will not let you be tried beyond your strength; but with the trial he will also provide a way out, so that you may be able to bear it" (10:13). Throughout my life, those words have meant so much to me.

When we returned home, our house was already filled with people. As we entered, more words from Scripture came to mind:

My sheep hear my voice; I know them, and they follow me. I give them eternal life, and they shall never perish. No one can take them out of my hand. My Father, who has given them to me, is greater than all, and no one can take them out of the Father's hand. The Father and I are one. (John 10:27-30)

Those words gave us the assurance that our daughter was in the arms of Jesus. As I have pondered this over the last thirty-seven years, God has given me many assurances that our daughter indeed is in his hands.

A remarkable incident occurred the day after Laura died. In the morning, Ray, a friend but not a close one at the time, appeared at the door and asked if he could come in. While I was reluctant to be meeting with people who were not close to us, I invited him in and asked, "What do you want?"

Ray said, "I don't want anything, but could I sit by myself in your dining room and pray?"

I said, "Fine."

And he sat there all day—in a corner, not interacting with anybody else in the house. The next day, he came back and asked if he could do the same thing. Through that experience, I realized that one of the greatest gifts of friendship is presence.

What Ray did is a great example of the reality of Jesus. His presence reminded us that Jesus is always with us, no matter what. This is true even if we do not realize it at the time.

From the beginning of our tragedy, the friends who constantly surrounded us gave us the strength to persevere. Without their friendship, I do not think we could have survived our loss. Friends from all over the country called us, wrote us, and, most important, prayed for us. Through them I learned a great deal about friendship with Jesus, his love for us, and friendship with others through him. I learned that authentic Christ-centered friendship is unconditional, compassionate, and caring.

Being totally helpless for the first time in my life taught me to rely more on others and allow my friends to be friends. I have come to know and experience the truth that real love from others changes everything. When I was deeply hurt, just feeling the love of friends made the pain bearable. I have never felt the presence of Jesus more profoundly than in the days, weeks, and months following Laura's death. As I began to travel around the country and speak again, telling this most important part of my story, I was amazed at how many people had suffered the loss of a child and how few had been comforted by friends the way we were.

Because of our friendship with Jesus, the relationship between Nancy and me deepened as we took comfort in the word of God—particularly in the Gospels and Psalms. I began to realize that Jesus would use Laura's life and our experiences in dealing with her death to bring others to the hope of Jesus.

When our daughter died, my pain was overwhelming. I couldn't sleep, nor could I think of anything else. However, the more I read Scripture, the more I felt the presence of Jesus in my mourning. Each night I would read Scripture before I went to sleep, and I would come across a passage that gave me an inner peace. I would then write our daughter's initials next to that passage, to remind me that Jesus was with me every step of the way in our journey of suffering.

As I have pondered whether or not Laura intended to take her life, I have come to the conclusion that she did not. Laura was a prolific note writer. If we went out for the evening and came back home, there would be a note on the bed with some expression of love or similar comment. If it was her intention to take her life, then she would have left a note to tell us why. In any case, I have total peace because I know where she is, and I know that we will someday join her.

I have also learned that deep suffering brings you closer to Jesus—if you are open to his unconditional love. You begin to understand, as never before, the true depths of his love for you, the love that led him to the cross so that we might be set free.

Personal Application

Take a few moments, either by yourself or in a small group, and reflect on the following questions. You can share your answers with others when you have finished your reflection.

1. How do you cope when something tragic or unforeseen happens in your life? What are some of the things that you hold on to during those difficult times?

2. How have friends helped you through the loss of someone close to you or assisted you through the grieving process? How have you been an authentic friend for someone else who has suffered a loss?

3. Have you ever thought about asking Jesus to help you through the difficult and tragic times in your life? If so, what happened when you did? If not, what is keeping you from asking Jesus to be present to you in your suffering?

CHAPTER 11

Friendships around the World

Six months after the death of our daughter, Nancy, Michael, and I took a monthlong trip to East Asia, visiting Japan, Thailand, and China. I thought it was necessary to create new memories for our family, particularly for our son, as well as for us to spend time as a family alone.

Doug Coe asked me to see a friend of his in Bangkok, whom he had met at the United States National Prayer Breakfast. I was not particularly interested in meeting with anybody outside the family during this trip. However, I thought I should make a courtesy call to this man, whose name was Chan Kornstrippa.

We arrived in Bangkok and checked in at the Oriental Hotel in the evening. As we were unpacking, the phone rang; it was Mr. Kornstrippa. He said that he had received a cable from Doug Coe about me and that he would pick us up at 8:00 a.m. the following morning. I told him that I was traveling with my family, and it would be wonderful to have lunch with him. But I did not want to impose on him, and the family really wanted to be alone.

He said, "Mr. Timmis, my car will pick you up at 8:00 a.m."

"Did you understand what I just said?" I asked.

He simply replied, "My car will pick you up at 8:00 a.m."

I looked at my wife helplessly (which is unusual for me), because Mr. Kornstrippa had hung up.

The next morning, we came down, and sure enough, there was a limousine waiting for us. That commenced one of the most incredible weeks of our lives. Mr. Kornstrippa took us all over Thailand. He insisted that we call him Chan, even though he would only refer to me as Mr. Timmis. If Michael inquired about something, Chan would tell his driver to go buy that for the boy. Chan took us to his home, a mansion in the middle of Bangkok surrounded by high walls. He had a ballroom in his house, complete with a disco ball for his many children.

The last night we were there, Chan insisted on having a banquet for us at a very nice hotel, and he invited several Thai government leaders. He even had a stage set up with seating. It was an amazing night. Toward the end of the dinner, I went up to the maître d and asked him to serve champagne to all the guests gathered so that I could make a toast. At the end of the dinner, I stood up and thanked the Kornstrippas for their time and kindness, and I expressed how grateful we were for their friendship.

When I finished the toast and sat down, Chan motioned me over to a corner and said, "Mr. Timmis, why did you do that?"

I replied, "Chan, you have been so generous to me and my family. I just wanted to acknowledge you in front of your friends."

He then said, "Mr. Timmis, I thought you were a Christian."

I replied, "Chan, you know I am."

That's when my host surprised me by saying, "A good Christian knows how to receive." It was a wonderful reminder. Chan gave me a great example of the power of authentic friendship.

About five years later, I was in Bangkok, meeting with the country's leaders and talking with them about Jesus. My hope was to help bring about reconciliation between opposing parties. I took the opportunity to go and visit the Kornstrippas because I knew that Chan had suffered a stroke. When I went to his house, I discovered that he was in a hospital bed in the living room, with many tubes attached to his body.

When I walked up to the bed, Chan started to shake, and I thought he was convulsing. But his wife told me that he shook like that when he was very happy. I could clearly see that my friend Chan was thrilled to see me. In that moment, I realized that God was allowing me to return an act of friendship to a man who had reached out to us at one of the most difficult times in our lives.

My wife and I were able to go back one more time to Bangkok, and I visited Chan once more. He had improved dramatically, and we could actually converse.

I have seen the results of being Jesus' friend and being friends with others all over the world. Being open and friendly, grounded in my love of Jesus, I have seen the Lord open many doors for me to walk through and touch the lives of others in his name.

The significance of friendship in Jesus was brought home to me when Nancy and I attended the International Congress on World Evangelization in Manila in 1989. At that time, I was on the board of Leighton Ford Ministries, which is dedicated to mentoring leaders in evangelism. Dr. Leighton Ford was the president of the conference.

The conference was held at a center outside the city. One day Nancy and I decided to leave early and return to our hotel in Manila. We walked to a bus stop, where we saw another man standing and waiting. He was Middle Eastern, and he asked where we were from. When we told him we were from the United States, he said, "My best friend lives in the United States. Maybe you know him?"

I smiled and said, "You realize there are approximately three hundred million people in the United States. Where does your friend live?"

He informed us that his friend lived in Washington, DC. Then I asked him his friend's name. I was almost bowled over when he told us his best friend was Doug Coe!

I laughed to myself because of the deep relationship Doug and I have. Not only was he my mentor and closest friend, but I knew he had this unique ability to immediately establish friendship with others through the power of the Holy Spirit. I saw this firsthand in the more than fifty countries that we traveled together to witness to leadership about reconciliation in Jesus.

Making a Friend

One year Nancy and I decided to go to the Pritikin Health Resort in Florida, to learn how to eat proper foods and generally improve our health. Many of our friends had gone there, and they told us that this would be a worthwhile experience. A group from Mexico was at the resort while we were there. They did everything together and pretty much kept to themselves.

One morning I got up early and went down to have breakfast at 6:00 a.m. One of the members of the Mexican group sat there at a table in the restaurant. Since no one else was dining in that place, I asked if I could sit with him and have breakfast. He agreed, and we started to talk.

He told me his name was Raymundo Leal and asked what I did for a living. I told him that I was a businessman and, along with my partner, owned a number of companies. His next question surprised me. "But what do you really do?" he asked intently.

No one had ever asked me a question like that. I said, "One of my passions is to go into prisons and tell prisoners about Jesus. I happen to be the chairman of Prison Fellowship International, the largest Christian organization reaching out to the incarcerated in the world."

He looked at me and asked if I was putting him on. When I asked him what he meant, he said, "I thought I was the only businessman who cared about prisoners. I have worked for years in Mexican prisons to rehabilitate prisoners in the name of Jesus." He continued, "I have purchased a defunct monastery and have trained ex-prisoners in a program that is extremely successful in rehabilitating drug addicts."

As he explained the program to me, I realized that it had the highest rate of success I had ever heard of. To my delight,

Raymundo invited me to Mexico to see his facility and the program.

The following Labor Day, I flew to Mexico City. Raymundo picked me up and drove me to his house in Cuernavaca. This was a beautiful estate in the middle of the city, surrounded by very high walls.

The more Raymundo and I talked, the closer we became. Like me, Raymundo was a daily communicant. He said the Rosary each day, as I do, and we read the same daily meditation book, *In Conversation with God* by Francis Fernandez.

Raymundo was a widower who had remarried. We eventually traveled together to Hong Kong, Malaysia, and China. He became an extremely close friend.

Raymundo had approached the governor of the state of Morelos and told him that if the state would give him a wing of a prison, he would totally refurbish it at his expense. The only requisite was that he could teach willing inmates about Jesus and the practical aspects of rehabilitation. The governor agreed. I had the privilege of attending the celebration marking the opening of the program. I spoke to the crowd through an interpreter and cut the ceremonial ribbon, formally opening that wing of the prison.

Raymundo became not only an extremely close friend but also a colleague, as he joined our International Board of Prison Fellowship. Meeting him proved to me once again the power of reaching out to a stranger in friendship and then seeing God's plan for that friendship unfold.

Unlikely Friends

Another good example of this occurred when I was visiting again in India with Mother Teresa, this time with Nancy. I went to meet with the head of the state of West Bengal, which contained approximately ninety million people. I had met him during another journey, when Doug Coe and I and a small group of friends went around the world evangelizing. This time I was alone.

The leader had cleared his schedule and was very happy to see me again. We quickly began to talk as friends. I shared with him some of the incredible breakthroughs of reconciliation I had seen in the name of Jesus. He started to laugh and said, "Michael, you forget that I am not a Christian. I am a Communist."

I said, "Well, I know you want to be a good Communist. Have you considered that I could be right about Jesus? And if so, knowing Jesus could help you help the people of the state of West Bengal."

I asked him if there was any man he could trust, and he told me that there was one man and that I reminded him of that man. I said, "Do you think you could pray with him?"

Just at that moment, the man in question walked into the office. The leader told him about what I had been saying about Jesus and reconciliation. I suggested that if the two of them would pray for reconciliation, wonderful things would begin to happen in their state.

I asked them if we could stand together. Then I put an arm around each of them and asked, "Is it all right if I pray for you and your leadership in the name of Jesus?"

I prayed as I have many times, asking Jesus to reveal himself to these men, to open their minds and hearts so that they could accept him as their Lord and Savior. It was a tremendous moment of unity, which I know deeply touched both men. This was only possible because we were talking about Jesus and friendship.

Personal Application

Take a few moments, either by yourself or in a small group, and reflect on the following questions. You can share your answers with others when you have finished your reflection.

1. Have you ever developed a surprise friendship with someone, one that emerged out of an unlikely situation or series of events? How did that friendship begin? How have you continued to nurture it through the years?

2. What do you think Chan Kornstrippa meant when he said, "A good Christian knows how to receive"?

3. Do you find it difficult to receive love, affirmation, kudos, or encouragement? What about gifts or attention from others? Why do you find it difficult, or why not?

4. Have you ever had the opportunity to speak to others about your friendship with Jesus? If yes, what happened? If not, does the thought excite you or fill you with fear?

CHAPTER 12

Friendship with My Son

Judging from what I've seen, most men do not have a clue about how to be fathers at the time their children are born. I have spoken numerous times around the country on the subject of fatherhood, particularly the relationship between fathers and sons, because I learned how to be a good father the hard way—through trial and error. It took many years for me to become a true friend to my son, and I wouldn't have been able to do so without bearing witness to the love, power, and presence of Jesus in my life and sharing that with him.

When Michael turned fifteen, he started to change. He became very cynical and rebellious, particularly toward me. I realized that with all my hard work and travel, I had been absent from home too often, and Michael thought he needed to be the man of the house. Now, with my newfound commitment to Jesus, I was changing. I started stepping up to try and live as the husband and father that God wanted me to be.

Rather than seeing this as a positive step, Michael was embarrassed by my commitment to Jesus.

I was happy when he went away to a Catholic university in Wisconsin. I thought it was a good choice because I had been told that it was a relatively conservative institution. I soon discovered, however, that it was the opposite.

The presence and political power of the breweries in Wisconsin at the time meant that an eighteen-year-old could drink beer legally. Students could buy beer in the student union. In addition, many of the professors were extremely liberal, holding values opposed to Catholic doctrine. Although Michael is very intelligent, he failed to perform academically, receiving mediocre grades. But he was having a great time.

One weekend Nancy and I went up north to enjoy the fall colors. We were at our summer home near a little town called Frankfort, along the shore of Lake Michigan. One of our best friends called to tell us that there was a big party going on at our house in Grosse Pointe Farms. I knew that our son was aware we were up north, but he was supposed to be at school in Milwaukee.

I was upset.

I called the Grosse Pointe Farms Police and told them someone was in my house throwing a party. If that someone identified himself as our son and said this was his home, I asked the police to inform that person that they had talked to me, and I had assured them that my son was in Milwaukee attending school. Therefore he must be an imposter, and everyone must leave the house in three minutes or be arrested.

A police sergeant then got on the line, and with a chuckle, he said, "Mr. Timmis, do you really want me to do that?"

I said, "Absolutely."

The police did exactly what I instructed. The sergeant called me back and laughingly told me that things had unfolded exactly as I had predicted. The house was cleared and locked up, and the police officer was thrilled. We never discussed what happened that night with our son. But I did take some small pleasure in the fact that Michael's plans were thwarted.

Needless to say, our relationship was rocky.

One Friday Michael came home from college, and we had a terrible argument. He told me that he hated me and everything that I stood for. In a moment of what could only have been grace, I told him that if he hated me, it was my fault and that I loved him with all my heart.

I prayed most of that night for Michael, and I gave him to my Father in heaven. I asked for only one thing: that Michael would be saved. I told the Father I didn't have to see it, but I wanted to know deep in my heart that it had happened. By morning I had a deep sense of peace.

That Sunday Nancy and I drove Michael to the airport. No one said a word the whole ride. Nancy and I had very heavy hearts. When we arrived at the airport, Michael got out, kissed his mother, said goodbye to her, and walked into the airport. I was so burdened by his lack of goodbye for me that I didn't immediately drive away.

Michael walked through the revolving doors and came back out. I told Nancy that he must have forgotten something. He came around to the driver's side, and I rolled down my window.

Michael leaned in without a word and gave me a kiss. It was the first step in a long process of reconciliation for us.

Michael told his mother and me that he was going to Daytona, Florida, with a group of friends during Easter break his senior year in college. Inasmuch as he was twenty-one years old, we didn't object. We were celebrating Easter at our then home on Sanibel Island in Florida with Doug and Jan Coe. During that Easter weekend, Michael called to tell us that he could not stand the living arrangements in Daytona, where he was sharing a room with six other guys. He chose to come and spend the time with us at our Sanibel condo.

Doug Coe had a tremendous ability to communicate with young people in a nonthreatening, Jesus-centered way. During dinner, he told us that he and some volunteers who assisted him communicated via regular mail with over two thousand people a month, sharing some thoughts about Jesus to encourage them. Michael asked Doug why he didn't have a computer to help him communicate with these people. Doug replied that he didn't have the time or the money to set up a computer to do that.

Michael said, "I could take your Rolodex and put it into a computer very easily, if you wanted me to do so after I graduate." So unbeknownst to Michael, I went out and bought a computer for Doug Coe.

After that weekend, Michael went back to school to finish his senior year. He returned home to Grosse Pointe in early June. Nancy asked him when he was going to Washington to help Doug Coe, but Michael responded that he was not going. "I don't want to be with a bunch of holy rollers" was his reply.

Nancy said that if that was the case, Michael needed to call Doug and tell him that he was breaking his word and not coming. Michael told his mother he couldn't do that, but she wouldn't let him off the hook. "Well," she said, "you are the one always criticizing hypocrites, and if you don't go, then you are a hypocrite."

Michael finally gave in and said, "OK, I'll go, but get me an open ticket, because I will be back in thirty-six hours."

Michael went to Washington, to a place called The Cedars, which is a large home near the Potomac River where many people come from around the world to spend time understanding and getting to know Jesus. Only Doug Coe would know to put Mike in a room with a black pastor from Soweto, South Africa, whose name was Nick Maputo. Sunday came, and Nick said, "Why don't you go to church with us?" Michael really did not want to go, but he begrudgingly assented.

Little did Michael know that he was about to attend a black Pentecostal Church, quite different from the Catholic parish of his youth. While he was in that church, God spoke to my son and told him to give Jesus all his pain. The Lord said that he would come into Michael's life and help him be whoever he wanted to be. Michael was never the same after that experience.

New Life

Michael stayed in Washington for approximately ten days and probably would have stayed longer. But before graduating from college, he had decided to spend a year in Africa serving the poor. He had to return home to receive the immunizations necessary for him to travel to Africa. Doug Coe called me before Michael left and told me that, although he had seen many young people converted to Jesus, he had never seen such a profound conversion as the one Michael experienced.

When Michael returned home, it was clear that he had changed. He started to read the Bible for up to eight hours a day and threw away all his heavy metal records. The transformation was absolutely unbelievable. Therefore it was difficult to see our only son go to Africa, to a country that had just experienced seventeen years of on-again, off-again civil war.

Michael's one year of service grew into something more; he would remain in Africa for seven years. Nancy and I bought a ranch of two and a half square miles, where Michael, along with two friends, established a Jesus-centered prep school for boys called Cornerstone Leadership Academy. Since those early days, CLA has affected thousands of lives through education, the building of homes, and many other projects. Even though Michael was over seven thousand miles away from us, we were closer than when he lived in Milwaukee. That was because of our shared love of Jesus.

One of the greatest gifts of my life has been to witness our son grow up to become one of my best friends and one of the finest men I know. After three and a half years in Africa, Michael married a beautiful, godly woman named Laura, who is like a daughter to us. She returned with Michael to Africa and lived with him there for another three and a half years. Michael recently completed ten years as chairman of the board of Ave Maria University.

Michael and Laura now have four daughters and one son, who happens to have Down syndrome. I have watched over the years as Michael has become a better husband and more caring father to our five grandchildren than I ever was to him. Michael and Laura have purposefully raised their children to be close friends with each other by praying together and resolving any differences by discussing them openly.

Our granddaughters are patient and loving toward our grandson. One day they told us that we didn't have to worry about Mikey's future because if anything ever happened to their parents, the four of them would each take Mikey for three months. And they would not marry anyone who did not love and accept Mikey.

Recently, I heard a friend speak about his journey in fathering his children. He said a father should first be an authoritarian to protect his children, and then as they get a little bit older, he should become a coach to them. Finally, as they mature, he should become their friend. I think that is a wonderful formula any father could follow.

I can truthfully say that Michael and I have become friends.

Personal Application

Take a few moments, either by yourself or in a small group, and reflect on the following questions. You can share your answers with others when you have finished your reflection.

1. What do you think of the stages of fatherhood (authoritarian, coach, friend) mentioned at the end of this chapter? Did you experience that progression with your own father?

2. What are some of the obstacles that exist between parents and children in regard to building friendship?

3. It is clear that a mutual shared love of Jesus can transform familial relationships. In what ways can families foster friendship with Jesus among their members?

CHAPTER 13

Cardinal Maida

One of the great friendships in my life came about in a very unusual way. Adam Maida was appointed archbishop of Detroit in 1990, succeeding Cardinal Edmund Szoka. Shortly thereafter, an acquaintance asked me if I would like to go boating on Lake St. Clair to the Old Club, which is on Harsens Island, for dinner with then Archbishop Maida and eleven or twelve other men. The boat was about sixty feet long, and while we cruised up to the island, I felt very uncomfortable. I made my way to the back part of the boat and sat by myself while the others socialized in the salon.

Suddenly Archbishop Maida came out and asked me why I was sitting there alone. I stood up and said, "I basically do not feel comfortable being here. None of these men are close friends of mine."

He replied, "Let me ask you a question. What do you think of the Catholic Church in Detroit?"

In my arrogance, I said, "Not much because there is no evangelization going on."

The archbishop asked if I was a practicing Catholic, and I told him that I attended Mass daily. He grabbed me by my shirt collar, pulled me up to his face, and said, "I don't think I'm anything special; come and talk to me."

That night I was saying my evening prayers, and I sensed that Jesus was upset with me. I felt him saying to me, "You pray every day for the evangelization of the people of the archdiocese, and when I gave you a chance to make a difference, you were arrogant."

I felt terrible. I asked God for forgiveness and pleaded with him to give me another opportunity with Archbishop Maida.

The next day I got a call from the archbishop's secretary, who said the archbishop wanted to meet me for breakfast the next day. I said, "Unfortunately I cannot because I am going out of the country."

There was a pause, then the secretary said, "Archbishop Maida wants to know when you will be back. He wants to see you the day after you get back."

That day came, and I drove down to the center of the city with some anxiety, thinking that I would be grilled by a number of priests. When I arrived at the archbishop's home, his secretary let me in and said, "The archbishop is waiting for you." Much to my surprise, the archbishop was sitting alone at his dining room table. Breakfast had been set out, and he said, "Sit down and eat."

I said, "Your Excellency, I know you do not have much time, so could I just talk to you?" When he indicated that would be OK, I shared my testimony about my relationship with Jesus and told him of my anxiety over the lack of evangelism in the archdiocese. He listened patiently and then told me to come work with him to help the poor. He said, "I will do any reasonable thing you ask of me, but do not embarrass me, because if you embarrass me, you are embarrassing the Church."

That started a tremendous friendship, and soon Nancy and the rest of my family came to love now Cardinal Maida. He baptized a number of our grandchildren, and he and his brother, Fr. Ted Maida, who also became a close friend, took many vacations with us in northern Michigan as well as in Florida.

I was on the board of Promise Keepers during this time, and I tried to persuade Cardinal Maida to allow me to organize a Promise Keeper-type event for Catholic men. He was reluctant, thinking it would not work, but eventually he relented. When we had our first event, it was standing room only. Cardinal Maida made an appearance, and he apologized to the men for not allowing these events earlier.

One of the highlights of our friendship occurred at a large event we had at the University of Detroit basketball stadium. I was scheduled to be the opening speaker. When I arrived, there was a chair by the podium, and I was asked to go and sit in the chair. Cardinal Maida came out to introduce me, and he talked for four or five minutes about what our relationship meant to him. I was deeply humbled.

At that time many Catholics did not understand why a layman was going around preaching the Gospel. Cardinal Maida understood the pushback I was receiving and said I needed credibility from the archdiocese. Eventually, he appointed me the president of the Archdiocese Endowment Foundation, a role I served in for twenty-five years.

My relationship with the Archdiocese of Detroit continues to this day with Archbishop Allen Vigneron, who succeeded Cardinal Maida. Archbishop Vigneron has instituted a tremendous evangelization outreach called "Unleash the Gospel," of which the purpose is to make every Catholic a "joyful missionary disciple."

Personal Application

Take a few moments, either by yourself or in a small group, and reflect on the following questions. You can share your answers with others when you have finished your reflection.

1. The author began a friendship with Cardinal Maida on a critical note, stating that there wasn't any evangelization going on in the Archdiocese of Detroit. How important is evangelization to your church or faith community?

2. What fruits have you seen from the evangelization efforts of your faith community? What fruits have you seen from your own evangelization efforts?

CHAPTER 14

Friendship
in Marriage

I believe a critical key to a successful marriage is becoming friends with your spouse. If a husband and wife do not become friends, it will be very difficult for them to maintain their marriage. I didn't always understand this, and it was only after I totally committed my life to Jesus and asked him to help me think, talk, and act like him that I began to understand friendship in marriage.

In the beginning of our marriage, I was very passionate and dedicated to my wife. However, as the newness of married life faded, familiarity set in. Once our children arrived and my excessive drive for success kicked into full gear, I made my marriage a secondary commitment. With a type A personality, I had many friends and often spent more time with them than I did with my wife.

It wasn't that I had fallen out of love with Nancy. In fact, she is the only woman I have ever loved. I had, however, started to take our marriage for granted. In the first twenty years of our marriage, I was a great provider but not a great husband.

Eventually, I recognized the signs of unhappiness in my wife and tried to do something about it—taking her on a weeklong trip to Europe, for example. We had many good experiences, but I was basically trying to put a Band-Aid on our marriage problems. Over time I learned that if you are not consistently available to your spouse, the marriage begins to diminish.

My biggest problem was the simple fact that I did not treat Nancy as a close friend; I kept her at a distance emotionally. I didn't want to share my career struggles with her, for example, because I didn't want to upset her. This was a huge mistake, as it shut her out of a big part of my life.

Before my conversion, I didn't really communicate with my wife well at all. Nancy used to say that sometimes she wished we lived in a car. When I asked her why, she replied that I only seemed willing to speak with her about important things when we were driving somewhere together.

When I committed myself to Jesus, I recommitted myself to our marriage. It was the grace I received through my friendship with Jesus that allowed me to actually change and become a better husband by becoming a better friend to Nancy. I sought to make amends for my neglect, changing my schedule and setting time apart each day so that we could talk with each other. That began a wonderful journey, which has continued over the last thirty-nine years and has brought us great happiness and fulfillment.

Praying together and studying Scripture have also become a bedrock of our marriage. These began when Nancy and I attended a couples' Bible study. We learned about unconditional love and tried putting that into practice in our marriage.

Though it obviously wasn't easy, the grace that we received through studying Scripture helped make it possible. The best thing about attending that Bible study was that, for the first time, we were doing something interesting and spiritual together.

As I observe the marriages of those whom I know, I see many of the mistakes that I made in my marriage. However, when I see spouses really attempting to act like Jesus, I see a total difference. That's why every other Tuesday night, my wife and I meet with four other couples to talk about some Christ-centered topic. It is a joyful time, when like-minded couples reinforce our belief in Jesus, friendship, marriage, and each other.

Jesus in Marriage

One of my greatest concerns for the future is the decline in marriage. Men and women do not understand that the purpose of marriage is more than sex and romance, but to become best friends and partners. When a couple live together without the benefit of the Sacrament of Marriage, they do not receive its sanctifying grace. They have not entered into a lifelong covenant with one another.

Statistics for 2020 demonstrate that approximately 50 percent of marriages result in divorce or separation. Millennials are saying no to marriage in record numbers. The median age for marriage is now twenty-seven for women and twenty-nine for men—up from twenty for women and twenty-three for men in 1960. A 2014 article in *Time* magazine was headlined "Why 25% of Millennials Will Never Get Married."[2]

Among the millennials choosing not to marry are probably many Christians who do not view the institution of marriage as a spiritual vocation rooted in Jesus. Part of this ignorance is due to the unleashing of sexual promiscuity in the sixties and the decades following, in which marriage and intimacy were no longer seen as related. One of the great reasons God gave us the gift of marriage is so that we could understand what true intimacy is. When a husband and wife join together in intimacy, there is the possibility of new life being created.

Likewise, when a man or woman commits their life totally to Jesus, a life-giving intimacy is born. This not only gives the individual new life but also offers that person the ability to give the life of Jesus to another. As Scripture teaches, "So whoever is in Christ is a new creation: the old things have passed away; behold, new things have come" (2 Corinthians 5:17). This new life of intimacy is a supernatural gift of grace. In the Sacrament of Holy Matrimony, God gives each of us a supernatural love for our spouse, which mirrors his love for us.

Looking more deeply at the parallels between friendship with Jesus and marital love reveals even more critical truths. Without communicating with Jesus daily and extensively, it is almost impossible to have a deep friendship with him. The more I communicate with Jesus, the more my friendship with him deepens. I have learned that whenever I am walking, waiting, or driving in the car, for example, I have an opportunity to silently converse with Jesus. Taking advantage of those moments deeply enriches my life.

Likewise, the more I communicate with my wife—taking advantage of opportunities to be present to her—the happier

and healthier our marriage becomes. This growth and transformation is intensified by the fact that both Nancy and I are
friends with Jesus, and he is the center of our marriage. Friendship with Jesus is the center of our marriage. When we end each
day, the three of us pray together: Jesus, Nancy, and I. This is
the prayer that we have said together for decades:

> Lord of night, Creator of the stars and moon, we thank you for
> the graceful gifts of this day. We rest in you, our divine friend
> and companion who watches over us while we sleep. May the
> pains and problems of today be healed as we place ourselves
> into your nightly care. Bless this evening those whom we love,
> and watch over them in a special way. Lord of day and night,
> of life and death, we place ourselves into your holy hands.

I have spoken of this practice many times to groups of men.
It is interesting how many men are afraid to pray with their
wives. My estimate is that over 90 percent of men never have.
When I sense their reluctance, I ask them if they are afraid to
show love to their wives.

Now, I know that is generally not the case, but nevertheless
men are hesitant to pray with their spouses. In my own case,
I found prayer to be incredibly healing. It removes any ten-
sion that arises in our relationship and helps Nancy and me
approach each other honestly and authentically.

A dear friend told me that he had started praying with his
wife every night before they go to sleep. Doing so, he said, had
an incredible effect on their marriage. So much so that when
he travels on business, his wife asks him to bless her before
he leaves for the trip.

Witnessing for Marriage

Two years ago, Nancy and I were in Uganda, East Africa, with a group of students who had graduated from Cornerstone and were attending the student chapel at Makerere University. They asked if we would like to go to Mass with them on Sunday. Obviously, we were pleased.

Makerere University has over fifty thousand students on a huge campus. In the middle of the campus are two churches, mirror images of each other—one Anglican and one Catholic. The interior of the Catholic church is shaped like a cross, and we sat on one arm of the cross, near the altar.

There were approximately eight hundred young people in attendance, and we were the only white people. It was one of the most beautiful Masses we were ever part of. The priest's homily was on the Sacrament of Holy Matrimony. When the priest finished the Mass and came down off the altar to give the final blessing, he looked over to where we were sitting and said, "See those two old white people there? You can tell they are in love."

He then said to us, "Would you come up on the altar?"

Somewhat reluctantly we did. The priest asked me how long we had been married, and I told him fifty-eight years. He said, "No, how long have you been MARRIED?" For some reason, he thought I was saying I was fifty-eight years old.

I said, "No, we have been married for fifty-eight years."

He said, "That's amazing." He then turned to the young people and exclaimed, "This couple has been married fifty-eight years!" (Fifty-eight years is almost equal to the average life expectancy of people in Uganda.)

He then asked me if I would tell him one of the secrets of our long marriage. I told him that it is all about Jesus. The more you love Jesus, the more you love your wife. And the more your wife loves Jesus, the more she loves her husband.

The priest looked at the young people and asked, "Did you hear what he said? It's all about Jesus. When you get married, it is all about Jesus."

When we left the church, a group of our former students at Cornerstone surrounded us. They were excited about what we had said. They recognized the truth: marriage is all about Jesus.

Personal Application

Take a few moments, either by yourself or in a small group, and reflect on the following questions. You can share your answers with others when you have finished your reflection.

1. In his Letter to the Ephesians, Paul exhorts spouses to submit to one another (see 5:21-25). What do you think authentic mutual submission looks like?

2. How does mutual submission relate to friendship? In what ways do friends submit to one another?

3. In what ways do you think mutual submission can lead to deeper friendship between spouses?

4. In what other ways can spouses help each other grow in their friendship with Jesus?

CHAPTER 15

Family of Friends

Following his graduation from Marquette University in 1988, Michael planned to head to Mozambique and travel with a pastor we knew who fed thousands of poor children. However, Doug Coe called and said someone in the US State Department believed that, with the civil war going on in Mozambique, Michael would probably be killed if he entered the country. Doug had an alternative: if Michael wanted to go to a very poor country in need, he should go to Uganda.

Doug had met a Ugandan named Gordon Wavamunno at the National Prayer Breakfast in Washington, DC. Gordon explained to Doug that Uganda had been decimated by an on-again, off-again civil war that had lasted seventeen years. The country was also one of the epicenters of the AIDS epidemic. Gordon asked Doug if he could help Uganda in some way.

Doug, who always thought out of the box, convinced Michael that he could help Uganda if he was open to the Holy Spirit. Michael, who was only twenty-two, went to South Africa for a couple of months and then moved into Gordon Wavamunno's home in Kampala, Uganda. Gordon was very generous, giving Michael a car to drive and overseeing his well-being.

When I look back on Doug's idea, it strikes me as a preposterous one. How could a twenty-two-year-old man with no experience help change Uganda? Michael had no vision of what he was going to do; he just had some vague idea about being a humanitarian.

Nancy and I visited a few months into Michael's stay. We met with Uganda's president, Yoweri Museveni, and Gordon Wavamunno. The president asked us to build a hospital in his home area, which had no medical facilities for the approximately 250,000 people who lived there. We agreed to do this. Michael, who had no experience in building, became the general contractor and built a hospital that is still in use today.

After Michael's first year in Africa, it became clear to Doug that Michael felt incredibly lonely in Uganda. So Doug asked another young man, John Riordan, to go to Uganda and become Michael's friend and partner. A short time later, another young man, Tim Kreutter, who was working with a ministry in the north of Uganda, became friends with Mike and John. That friendship eventually blossomed into a partnership.

Tim Kreutter and his wife, Cathy, had lived most of their married life in Africa, working in different ministries. Tim's father and mother were missionaries in Africa; his mother had died in an automobile accident in the Congo. Tim had deep feelings for and understanding of Africa.

One of the things that drew Tim into friendship with Michael and John was the fact that he had been raised a Baptist, and the other two men were Catholic. Tim thought it would be extremely important for the three of them to represent unity in Jesus for a country that had been so divided.

Because of the war and the AIDS epidemic, there were a huge number of orphans in Uganda. Originally, our son thought of building several orphanages. However, as the friendship among the three men deepened, their passionate discussions about the country convinced them that education was the most important need at that time. School fees were so expensive that most children dropped out before finishing their elementary education.

Michael approached us and told us of their decision. He asked if we would buy a so-called ranch, consisting of two and a half square miles and thus offering plenty of room for expansion. The ranch was about two hours north of Kampala, in an area called the Luwero Triangle. This was the site of some of the worst atrocities during the prolonged Ugandan civil war.

Nancy and I agreed, and I went to Uganda to see the property. When I arrived, I felt that I had been somewhat misled. The ranch was mostly wild bushland, with about a hundred skinny cows that looked as if they were about to die. I thought I had made a horrible mistake in buying this property. However, our son cleared the land in about a year and started to build a high school there, which they called Cornerstone.

Uganda follows an old British system in education. Before someone can attend a university, they have to complete what is called Senior Five and Six, which correspond to grade twelve and the first year of college in the United States. Most Ugandans cannot afford to go that far in school because of the expensive school fees. Michael, John, and Tim would make the school free, which would attract many potential students.

One of Cornerstone's main principles was to promote tribal unity in the Spirit of Jesus. The school would take no more than two or three students from a given tribe. Michael, John, and Tim solicited candidates for the school from priests, pastors, and ministers around the country.

The three young men wanted to create a school that would strive for educational and spiritual excellence. It would be a kind of prep school, so that students could move on to higher education and become agents of change and leaders for their country. (Anyone in Uganda who graduated from a university would automatically be in the country's top 5 percent in terms of influence.)

The first class consisted of twenty-five male students. That year presented a number of obstacles due to tribal and religious differences and to the fact that Michael, John, and Tim were neophytes in establishing a school. To our knowledge, nobody had ever tried to bring together such a diverse group of students and lead them into a relationship with Jesus so that they could become friends and brothers in Christ in an environment of educational excellence.

I went to Uganda for the first graduation, and I met a young man who had really struggled in his two years at Cornerstone. I talked with him about what those two years meant. He said that before he got there, he didn't think anybody could be a close friend unless he was a member of his tribe. He learned at Cornerstone that there is only one tribe, the tribe of Jesus. So all his fellow students had become his brothers and his friends. That was the moment I realized that we had an opportunity to lift up Jesus to the people of East Africa.

After three and a half years, Michael came home. Following a lengthy long-distance relationship, he was ready to marry a young Christian woman named Laura Gagnon. They returned to Uganda for another three and a half years. Michael's one-year commitment thus turned into seven years. Then he and Laura determined that they wanted more education, so they returned to the United States and earned MBAs from the University of Michigan.

John Riordan married a young woman from Australia named Margaret Cameron, who had visited Cornerstone. For a time they both lived on the ranch and deeply influenced the students there.

Tim Kreutter became the director of the work in Uganda. Through his tremendous leadership and vision over the years, we have established three schools on the ranch: a boys' academy, a coed community high school with boarding, and an elementary school. In total there are over fifteen hundred students attending the schools on the ranch, with many of them living there in dormitories.

The boys' school was so successful and recognized in the country that we decided to create a girls' high school closer to Kampala, following the pattern of the boys' school. At the same time, we wanted to strengthen the unity of all our graduates, and so we created an alumni group, Cornerstone Old Students Association (or COSA). Tim Kreutter started to make public the term "Family of Friends," to project to the world what the work of Cornerstone was all about.

Reconciliation through Jesus

That Family of Friends continued to grow. Cornerstone graduates established a number of separate homes for boys and girls, where children as young as nine or ten were taken off the street, clothed, fed, nurtured, and given the love of Jesus. The schools proved so successful that—through a number of circumstances, particularly the generosity of our dear friends Ronnie and Nina Cameron—we built a coed high school in Rwanda. Our desire was to deepen the reconciliation between the two tribes in this country.

In 1993, Rwanda experienced a genocide, in which close to a million Tutsi men, women, and children were slaughtered in a period of approximately one hundred days. The Hutus, the other major ethnic group in Rwanda, led this slaughter. They were eventually overthrown by a Tutsi army from Uganda. That army installed a Tutsi leader named Paul Kagame as president of the country. Immediately he outlawed the use of the ethnic terms "Hutu" and "Tutsi."

The Rwandan school was a little different from our schools in Uganda. Not only was it larger, but it conformed to the educational system in Rwanda, encompassing three years of school rather than two. Over time this school has accomplished tremendous reconciliation between peoples in this still-wounded country. And for the last three years, our school has been the number one academic high school in Rwanda.

Ronnie Cameron and I have become close friends over these many years, and he is probably the most generous man I have ever met. It was at his urging and generosity that we were able to expand not only into Rwanda but also into Tanzania. We found land near Arusha, Tanzania, and built a school patterned on the Rwandan coed school, with about 150 students.

Another foundation asked Cornerstone's help in establishing a school in South Sudan. War had raged in Sudan for many years, eventually leading to the separation of the northern and southern regions of the country. After the separation, another war started between two tribes, the Nuer and the Dinka. Following the pattern we have established through the years, we are attempting to bring academic excellence and reconciliation in South Sudan through Jesus. Our school is the only one of its kind in the country.

Altogether the schools, homes, and programs we have established serve more than two thousand young people at any given time. This includes our schools in Uganda, Rwanda, Tanzania, and South Sudan, as well as our work with young people in the Congo, Burundi, and Kenya.

One of the most important aspects of Cornerstone has been the continued development and nurturing of our alumni group, COSA. Over the past twenty-five years, we have managed to stay in touch with close to 90 percent of our graduates. This is facilitated through newsletters, retreats, social media, and individual contacts. We see living proof that friendships can be built across nations in accordance with the teachings of Jesus and as a result of friendship with him.

Through the perseverance and leadership of Tim and Cathy Kreutter, the concept of Family of Friends has spread throughout East Africa and found great favor among its leaders. What we have proclaimed is friendship with Jesus and friendship with others because of Jesus. This has been so well received that we are affecting thousands of young people in East Africa and beyond. Such is the leadership of Tim Kreutter and the deep friendship among the two hundred-plus young leaders of Cornerstone, almost all of whom have attended Cornerstone schools or one of our other projects.

Personal Application

Take a few moments, either by yourself or in a small group, and reflect on the following questions. You can share your answers with others when you have finished your reflection.

1. Was there ever a time in your life when you struggled with a sense of loneliness and isolation? How did you move through that experience?

2. Clearly the friendship of Michael, Tim, and John strengthened and inspired them to say yes to Jesus and follow through on the Cornerstone initiative. In what ways have your friendships with others strengthened you in your personal or professional life?

3. In what ways has your friendship with Jesus inspired or called you to serve others? How have you acted on those inspirations?

4. Have you ever been friends with someone whose social standing, ethnicity, belief system, or other attribute made your family or social circle upset, nervous, or uncomfortable? How has your friendship influenced others' perception of your friend?

CHAPTER 16

New Canaan Society: Friendships with Men

A number of years ago, I was asked to speak to a group of men in New Canaan, Connecticut, at the home of the group's founder, Jim Lane. Jim's parents, James, Sr., and his wife, Arlyne, had been friends with Nancy and me for many years, as we were part of a small prayer group in Grosse Pointe, Michigan. It was through the senior Lanes that I met their son Jim.

When I inquired about this group called the New Canaan Society (NCS), I learned its mission and purpose:

NCS is a network of men joined by a common desire for a deep and abiding friendship with Jesus, and lasting and transparent friendships with each other. The mission and purpose of NCS is to connect men who seek and value such friendships, to work together in partnership and to encourage and equip each other to experience personal transformation, in an environment of trust and acceptance. Through friendship, partnership and transformation, we will have a positive and powerful impact on our families, our communities, the marketplace and the world.[3]

I love the motto of NCS, "Live Pure, Speak Truth, Right Wrong, Worship the King."[4] It would be a number of years before I spoke at different NCS chapters. I discovered that all men are welcome, despite background, race, religion, politics, and so on. NCS meets in places like restaurants, offices, and homes. Interestingly, the group is not a Bible study, prayer meeting, or Christian support group. Even more astounding, there are no dues or fees.

For many years I had met with men who are lonely and isolated. But with the press of my own personal life and business, I found it extremely hard to follow up with them, particularly when they were out of state. When I learned that there was a place to which I could direct men to meet with other men in a spirit of Jesus, it truly gladdened my heart.

Today NCS is an international movement of thousands of men who meet to encourage each other in friendship and faith in an effort to become better fathers, husbands, and leaders in the marketplace and their communities. Approximately fifty chapters meet weekly or biweekly around the country, in twenty-six states. And men have formed chapters in London, England, and Kampala, Uganda, with men in other countries ready to follow suit.

In Grosse Pointe, Michigan, where I have lived most of my married life, my friend Ed Russell and I formed a chapter of NCS, which Ed has developed and leads. Dozens of men come to our meetings each week. As I write this, we are beginning to meet again in person instead of on Zoom, which we did during the height of the COVID-19 pandemic. We come together regularly to share friendship with one another, tell our stories, and experience fellowship. During these meetings, we have discovered that hearing a man's simple story is just as important as hearing from someone who has survived a crisis or is super successful. We try to avoid displaying any spiritual superiority.

John's Story

One of the greatest examples of NCS's effectiveness can be seen in the story of a man whom I will call John, due to the guarantee of confidentiality that is a value of our meetings. I knew John for over twenty-five years. Over that time, I invited him to retreats and Bible studies, but he never showed any interest. John was an extremely intelligent, successful, and wealthy businessman.

One day John showed up at our Grosse Pointe NCS meeting, and soon he started to attend on a regular basis. However, he pretty much kept to himself. At one of our meetings, he was asked to do the closing prayer, and he replied, "Absolutely not."

About a year and a half before John started coming to our meetings, a friend named Chip came to speak to the chapter. Chip had an extremely interesting background. A businessman, he had started a company and taken it public. But he was convicted of insider trading and ultimately went to prison.

Just before Chip went to prison, he met some of the brothers from the New Canaan Society, and they surrounded him with friendship—going so far as to drive him to the prison when he started his incarceration. While he was in prison, he met an African American man who likewise was a businessman, and they became fast friends. Their friendship, rooted in Jesus, quickly expanded to include dozens of men who were also seeking friendship through Jesus.

When Chip and his friend were released from prison, both started to speak to various NCS chapters around the country about their experience. Chip came to speak to the Grosse Pointe chapter when John was present. Chip brought three of his African American brothers who had served time with him in prison. During the question-and-answer period at the end of the talk, John said, "I wish I could flip a switch and believe what you believe."

Chip replied, "All you have to do is to do it." He then knelt down in front of John, who was seated, and asked a Catholic priest who was a member of the chapter to put his hands on John's shoulders. Chip then prayed for John to receive Jesus, and all of a sudden, John raised his hands and said, "I believe." The rest of the men gathered around John and, with tears in their eyes, prayed for him.

Sometime later, John contracted cancer and had a difficult time getting to our meetings. About two months after his diagnosis, he appeared at a meeting and asked if he could say something at the end. John knew that the men had been praying for him, which he deeply appreciated.

John told his story about growing up in a family with no faith. During the summers, he would visit his grandparents, who said the Lord's Prayer before each meal. John admitted that this had impressed him greatly throughout all those years, as the memory remained with him. He recalled that a year and a half earlier, he had been asked to say a prayer at the end of our meeting but had not been ready to. Now, he said, he wanted to pray.

So very simply and humbly, John thanked God for the friendships he had made at NCS. He shared how much it meant to him. The men surrounded John and thanked him for his faith and friendship.

John died soon thereafter. His wife wrote a note to us: "I am so glad he went to the Wednesday meetings with all of you. He really needed the friendship he found there. And you all helped him believe in the Lord. He truly enjoyed the thoughts and prayers."

John's experience at NCS is not unique. We have found that most men working in the marketplace feel isolated, alone, and often overwhelmed by the pressures and temptations that they experience. NCS is a place where men can form deep friendships and experience real growth in Jesus. This is done by creating an environment where all men are made welcome, no matter what they do for a living or what mistakes they have made in their lives. Our speakers, all followers of Jesus, share the stories of their journeys through life with the intention of inspiring and encouraging others.

To sum it all up, the New Canaan Society is probably the greatest movement of friendship among men that I have experienced. There is a brotherhood that crosses every conceivable division, because ultimately, friendship with Jesus leads to friendship with others because of Jesus. I have had the privilege of serving on the national board of NSC for the last six years, watching with great joy its incredible growth among men.

Personal Application

Take a few moments, either by yourself or in a small group, and reflect on the following questions. You can share your answers with others when you have finished your reflection.

1. Have you ever had the opportunity to be a part of a men's or women's group focused on fellowship and friendship in Jesus? If yes, what was that like? If you haven't, what has kept you from doing so?

2. Have you ever felt isolated, alone, or overwhelmed by the pressures and temptations of working in the marketplace? How did you deal with them? How might a group like the New Canaan Society help you deal with those issues?

3. Do you think it is harder or easier today than it was twenty years ago to live as a Christian in the public sphere? Why?

4. What are some ways you might help build bridges of friendship between yourself and those in society who believe differently than you do?

5. How might your friendship with such people open them up to friendship with Jesus?

CHAPTER 17

Friendship in Prison

Looking back on my life, one of the greatest blessings I see is over thirty years of involvement with those who are incarcerated. In 1990, Chuck Colson, the head of Prison Fellowship International (PFI) and someone I had become quite close to, asked me to join the board.

In conversation, Chuck had asked me what God's call on my life was. I told him it was for the poor. He asked me a question that surprised me at first: "Who do you think are the poorest of the poor?"

Now, Nancy and I had visited a lot of places where people were poor, and I told Chuck just that. He wasn't satisfied with my answer. He pressed on. "The poorest are those who are in prison, because they have lost their lives, their families, and in many cases their dignity."

I was still not moved. We were already working with the very poor in Honduras, Peru, and Nicaragua, as well as in Uganda in conjunction with our son, Michael.

It was Chuck's thoughts on unity that captivated my mind and heart. Chuck and Fr. Richard Neuhaus were establishing a movement of Evangelicals and Catholics together. Chuck said to me, "You are a Roman Catholic leader, and I am a Southern Baptist leader, and together we could represent to the world that we are united as brothers in Jesus." It was for this reason that I joined the board of Prison Fellowship US, not fully realizing that this was all part of God's plan to change me into the man he created me to be.

Seven years later, Chuck stepped down as chairman of Prison Fellowship International and asked me to take his place. I did that, while remaining on the board of Prison Fellowship US. By that time I had traveled to dozens of countries with Doug Coe, meeting with presidents, prime ministers, and other political leaders in order to spread the concept of reconciliation in Jesus. In my dual roles within Prison Fellowship, I continued such meetings but also visited those who were least, last, and lost in prisons, both in the US and abroad.

I realized that those who are in prison are also made in the image and likeness of God—just like me. Furthermore, I grew in my conviction that Jesus loves them and died for them, as he had for me, and that he wanted them to inherit eternal life. Throughout my time meeting and speaking to those in prison, I discovered that the only true message that really resonates with people is that of friendship.

This was illustrated graphically when Chuck and I obtained permission to go to Huntsville, Texas, and speak to prisoners on death row. Huntsville is where all executions in the state of Texas take place. Chuck took one cellblock, and I took another.

As you might imagine, death row is an extremely depressing place. The prisoners are in what is called "lockdown," a very narrow cell no more than five or six feet wide. Throughout my visit, on each side of me, I had a guard armed with a shotgun. This was frankly intimidating—and unnecessary.

Whenever I visit prisoners, I always give my first name and ask the prisoner if I can speak with them. In Huntsville I came to the cell of an African American man and stopped and asked to speak to him. The man said his name was King and that he had not had a visitor in three and a half years. He was scheduled for execution. King told me to move along. He, a black Muslim, wasn't interested in talking to any white Christian.

I asked King if he was a true Muslim, and he said yes. I then said that if he read the Quran, as I had, then he would know that we had something tremendous in common. He asked me what that was. I said, "Friendship with Jesus." I knew that the Quran mentioned Jesus more than Muhammad.

I then explained to King my friendship with Jesus. I asked him if he had a Bible. He said he did, because everyone on death row is given one, but he had never read it. I said that as a good Muslim, he might like to know who Jesus was, who he said he was, what he said, and what he did. I suggested that if he read John's Gospel, which he could find by opening up to the index of the Bible, he could learn all these things about our mutual friend, Jesus.

I told King I had to move on, but I asked him if I could pray for him in the name of Jesus. He agreed. I closed my eyes and, without thinking, raised my hands (which is the way Muslims often pray). I prayed out loud that Jesus would reveal himself to King and that King would come to know that he was loved and forgiven. Furthermore, I prayed that my brother would accept Jesus as his Lord and Savior.

While I prayed, King thrust his hands through the bars and held my hands tightly. It was one of the most profound moments of my life. I realized that if I had not come simply as a friend of Jesus who extended friendship to this man in his name, King would not have listened to me.

Introducing My Best Friend

As I mentioned above, after I introduce myself as Mike to the prisoners I visit, I ask for their permission to speak with them. I have done this throughout the thirty years of my prison ministry. Often these prisoners will say no, they are not interested. When that happens, I simply inquire if I can ask them one question. They generally respond with a yes. When they do, I ask them this question: "Why the hell do you think I want to talk to you? You're in prison, and I'm free. I could be doing anything else I wanted to do besides talking to you in this terrible place."

This tends to rouse their curiosity, and they generally respond by asking, "Why *do* you want to talk with me?"

That is when I tell them that a friend of theirs has sent me to see them. Almost every time they ask, "Who would you know that I know?"

I respond by saying my best friend sent me. And he really wants to be your best friend. His name is Jesus, and while you know his name, you probably don't know anything about him.

I have never had anyone refuse to talk with me.

I share this to drive home a point: if someone sees you as a real person who truly cares about serving Jesus, you will have a chance to break through the façade of toughness that every prisoner projects.

Through God's calling, my work with Prison Fellowship International (PFI) allowed me to lift up Jesus to prisoners throughout the world. It also brought me into a lifelong friendship with the godly Ron Nikkel, who was president of PFI for thirty-two years. I believe that Ron has been in more prisons around the world than any person on the planet. Through our friendship, we became brothers in the expansion of God's love for prisoners all over the world.

As I started going to Uganda once or twice a year, in addition to visting Cornerstone, I decided to start visiting prisons. For almost twenty years, I visited death row to share my friendship with Jesus. One day, I was informed that twenty-nine men had been executed in a single day. When I heard about this, I went to Uganda to meet with President Yoweri Museveni in his home area of Rushere. He and I had a long talk.

I knew he wanted to be recognized for the incredible repatriation of refugees that he had brought back to Uganda after the civil war. I pointed out that the execution of twenty-nine prisoners was extremely disturbing to leaders in the West. If he wanted to be taken seriously by world leaders, he would have to stop these mass executions.

Since that time, no one else has been executed by the state of Uganda. Through the efforts of Prison Fellowship and others, the law has been changed so that anyone who is not executed within three years will be released into the general population of the prison. A great number of prisoners have been removed from death row.

Prison Fellowship Academy

Four years ago, a businessman named James Ackerman became president and CEO of Prison Fellowship Ministries (US). James felt a call from Jesus to leave an extremely lucrative position in business and take over leadership of Prison Fellowship. Prior to James's coming, the effectiveness of Prison Fellowship had begun to diminish. James brought an exciting new perspective, increased morale, and made it an extremely dynamic ministry once again.

About a year after James took leadership, he called me for advice. He expected me to be somewhat upset because no one had contacted me since I left the board. However, I was so taken by him, even though we had not yet met, that there was an instant chemistry between us.

Subsequently, Nancy and I had the opportunity to meet with James and his lovely wife, Martha. James eventually asked if I, along with a brother in California named Rick Osgood, would commit to being prayer partners with him and hold him accountable in all areas of his life. This was a mark of an incredible friendship, and that friendship continues to this day.

Prison Fellowship is now reaching approximately five hundred thousand prisoners in forty-nine states with various programs. I am very pleased that they are using the Alpha course (detailed in the next chapter) as part of their outreach to inmates.

One of James Ackerman's major innovations is the establishment of the Prison Fellowship Academy. In select prisons across the country, Prison Fellowship has established this intensive biblically-based program, which offers incarcerated men and women a holistic life transformation. Prison Fellowship staff and volunteers guide participants to lives of purpose and productivity inside and outside of prison.

As a cornerstone program of Prison Fellowship, the academy guides participants to identify the life-controlling issues that led to their incarceration and take responsibility for their impact on their community. Using biblically-based materials, the academy specifically targets criminal thinking and behavior, life skills, addictions, victim impact, and prosocial culture change. Prisoners who have leadership potential are trained to serve as positive peer mentors and supporters of a positive culture based on Gospel values. Those who complete the program and are preparing for release have the opportunity to connect to post-release resources and support in metropolitan areas.

The Prison Fellowship Academy is the most revolutionary movement in the world to help the those who are incarcerated, those whom society often considers to be the least, last, and lost.

Personal Application

Take a few moments, either by yourself or in a small group, and reflect on the following questions. You can share your answers with others when you have finished your reflection.

1. One of the basic principles of Christian friendship is that no one is beyond the grace, love, mercy, and redemption of God, no matter what they have done. Have you ever tried to begin or maintain a friendship with someone who was unpopular, an outcast, or someone written off by society? If yes, what was that experience like? If no, what would it take for you to begin such a friendship with one of the "least, last, and lost"?

2. Those who are imprisoned seem far away from us in terms of social standing and morality. We tend to forget that all of us fall far short of God's perfection, and he loves us still. If Jesus can love us to his death—despite our sins, failures, and flaws—and invite us to true friendship with him, what might he ask us to do in relation to those living on the fringes of society? How should we approach those who are the "least, last, and lost?"

CHAPTER 18

Friendship with Jesus through Alpha

In my last years as chairman of Prison Fellowship International, I met many prisoners all over the world who had taken a course called Alpha. What I saw greatly impressed me: men and women were entering into deep friendship with Jesus through this process. I learned that Alpha started at Holy Trinity Brompton, an Anglican Church in London. Nancy and I decided to go to London, where Alpha was holding a global conference, and observe what it was all about.

We discovered that Alpha is a ten–to-eleven-week course that leads people into a personal encounter with Jesus through the power of the Holy Spirit. Alpha presents a series of sessions exploring who Jesus is and what it means to follow him. It creates a space, online or in person, where people can bring their friends for a nonthreatening conversation about faith, life, and God.

Alpha began at Holy Trinity Brompton (HTB) in 1977 through the work of the then curate, Charles Marnham. In

1990, Nicky Gumbel became chairman of Alpha and repositioned Alpha as a course for those outside the church. It quickly attracted the attention of hundreds of people.

The Alpha team realized that there were many outside the church who wanted to explore the Christian faith. This led to the first Alpha conference at HTB in 1993, drawing over a thousand church leaders to learn about Alpha and how to use it in their church communities. As interest in Alpha grew, the team organized international conferences. They developed the original Alpha Film Series in 1994, to make it accessible to a wider audience.

The courses consist of the following sessions:

Week 1: Is There More to Life Than This?
Week 2: Who Is Jesus?
Week 3: Why Did Jesus Die?
Week 4: How Can I Have Faith?
Week 5: How and Why Do I Pray?
Week 6: Why and How Should I Read the Bible?
Week 7: How Does God Guide Us?
Week 8: How Can I Resist Evil?
Week 9: Why and How Should We Tell Others?
Week 10: Does God Heal Today?
Week 11: What about the Church?

Each evening begins with a meal and low-key fellowship, followed by a brief talk on the topic of the evening and small group discussion.

When Nancy and I arrived at the Alpha conference at Holy Trinity Brompton, we were amazed to see how many people we knew from our travels with Prison Fellowship and through the National Prayer Breakfast. I felt a sense of spiritual unity that I had never felt before. Somebody mentioned to Nicky Gumbel that the chairman of Prison Fellowship International was in attendance. He asked me to come up on stage and share some of my observations of what Jesus was doing in prisons of the world and why I had come to this conference.

About three months later, I received a call from Nicky Gumbel, who at that time was also the vicar of HTB. He asked if I would consider joining the board of Alpha International, because he felt they needed a Roman Catholic leader. I accepted the invitation, and I have served on the board of Alpha International for over ten years.

I have served on many Christian boards, and no organization embraces unity in the way that Alpha has around the world. Every mainline denomination has participated. And while I have served on many Evangelical boards that were open to Catholics, none have embraced Catholics as Alpha does. They see Catholics as true partners and friends in the mission of evangelizing the world.

One of the things that Nicky asked me to do was to help get Alpha established in the Catholic Church in America. There had been some attempts—there was a foothold in the Boston area, for example—but Alpha had not really spread from there. I realized that the Catholic Church is reluctant to embrace movements that do not originate from the Catholic world. I knew therefore that there had to be clergy oversight.

After talking to some friends in the Archdiocese of Detroit, I met with an ordained deacon, Steve Mitchell, and asked him to become executive director of Alpha in a Catholic Context (ACC) in the US. We formed an advisory board, and I became chairman. We began to spread the Alpha course throughout Catholic churches in North America.

Steve did a tremendous job for seven years. In 2016 the leadership of ACC passed on to Josh Danis, who has organized and advanced the cause of Alpha across the country. The Archdiocese of Detroit became a leader in the number of parishes running the Alpha course. It helped immeasurably when Auxiliary Bishop (now Archbishop) Michael Byrnes joined the board of directors of Alpha USA.

Throughout the world, almost thirty million people have taken the Alpha course. It has been translated into 112 languages, and the Alpha talks have been repackaged for today's audience in a new Alpha Film Series. The Alpha Youth Series was created to reach the younger generation. Even as times have changed, churches have continued to find the Alpha course an effective tool for reaching those who are lost with the gospel of Jesus Christ.

Alpha now runs in every part of the global church, including the Catholic Church, the Orthodox Church, and all mainline and independent Protestant churches. Although Alpha USA was birthed in the 1990s, only in the last few years has the course been widely used by every mainline denomination. Last year in the United States, 425,000 people took the Alpha course, and approximately 140,000 of those participants were Catholic.

In talking with Christians all over the country, I have been surprised that so few people have had any personal encounter with Jesus and thus have never entered into a friendship with him. This is true both with Catholics and Protestants. I believe many priests will agree with me that while Alpha is not the only evangelization course, it certainly is one of the most successful in leading Catholics into a personal friendship with Jesus.

Archbishop Allen Vigneron has made the evangelization of Catholics in the Archdiocese of Detroit one of his greatest priorities. He encourages every Catholic to become a joyful missionary disciple. There is no way anyone can do that without having a deep personal friendship with Jesus.

As I mentioned previously, I have also become involved with Prison Alpha, which is headquartered in London. A few years ago, we established in the United States an advisory board for Prison Alpha, of which I am a member. Under the leadership of Jack Cowley, a former warden, and with a limited budget, we established Alpha courses in approximately 650 prisons, pre-COVID-19 pandemic. True rehabilitation occurs when a person has a change of heart, and this occurs when someone meets Jesus through the Alpha course.

Being on the board of Alpha International, as well as the advisory boards of Alpha in a Catholic Context and Prison Alpha, has been one of the great privileges of my life. I see friendship with Jesus and a spirit of unity expanding in an unprecedented way.

One unique thing about the Alpha course, and now the Alpha Marriage Course, is that it is free. There is no solicitation of money from those who are taking the Alpha course, which makes it possible for Christian communities to offer it to people across the socioeconomic spectrum. Jesus transforms lives through his friendship, which people come to experience through programs like Alpha.

Personal Application

Take a few moments, either by yourself or in a small group, and reflect on the following questions. You can share your answers with others when you have finished your reflection.

1. Do you have a place in your life—at home, at work, in church, or out in the community—where you find it easy and nonthreatening to talk about things of faith with others? If yes, what is that place, and how has having that space impacted your life? If no, would you hang out in that kind of space if one existed for you?

2. Why is unity within the Church, between the various members of Christ's body, so important? In what way do you think our unity, or lack of unity, affects our witness to the world?

3. The Alpha course is just one way in which individuals can hear the gospel of Jesus Christ. If someone asked you to share the basic message of the gospel, how would you respond?

4. How might you help someone respond to Jesus' invitation to friendship?

5. Have you ever had the opportunity to speak to others about your friendship with Jesus? If yes, what happened? If not, would you say that the thought excites you or fills you with fear?

CHAPTER 19

Friendship through Unity

After Nancy and I had really committed our lives to Jesus, we started to examine our relationships with our friends and the community. We realized how many men and women we knew who were just like us: they were trying to be successful, but their marriages were not particularly happy.

There was basically no evangelization going on in our community. Both Nancy and I felt a strong prompting to change that. We had friends and acquaintances who we knew were really sold out to Jesus. So seven couples got together and started to pray monthly for our churches and our community at large.

Three couples were Catholic, and four were Evangelical. But all of us were in total unity because of our belief in Jesus. We called ourselves the Host Couples because we did not want to present any labels other than friendship with Jesus. We operated on the principle that *in essentials, unity; in nonessentials, liberty; in all things, love.*

For thirty-one years, the Host Couples sponsored an annual business retreat. We would bring in Bible teachers from around the country, present testimonies, pray, and socialize, with the hope of deepening everyone's relationship with Jesus.

As a result of the decades-long commitment of the Host Couples, evangelism came to be accepted in all our local churches. Many prayer groups and Bible studies were established and continue to this day. This would not have been possible without the deep friendships that developed among the members of the Host Couples.

Many years ago, a prayer breakfast started in the Grosse Pointe, Michigan, communities. My friend John Boll and I attended, and to say it was Christian-lite would be an understatement. We went to the mayors of the five small cities involved and said we would be willing to take over the planning and organizing of the event. We have done this for thirty years, bringing in outstanding speakers from around the state and country.

Additionally, we were concerned about children in high school because both drugs and sexual promiscuity were epidemic in our schools. As a father who had teenagers, I was particularly concerned. I asked Peter Moore, the head of FOCUS (Fellowship of Christians in Universities and Schools), to allow FOCUS to be organized in Grosse Pointe. This FOCUS—not to be confused with another great group, the Fellowship of Catholic University Students, founded by Curtis Martin— was a movement centered on East Coast, private, Episcopal boarding schools.

At first FOCUS was reluctant to expand from private schools to a community-based ministry. However, we persisted, and they finally said they would come. We offered to support a couple who would minister to the kids. We had FOCUS in our community for many years; then the board decided that they wanted to limit their activities again to the boarding schools.

Then we partnered with Young Life, another Christian organization that focuses on ministry to preteens and teens. Our FOCUS board transitioned smoothly into a Young Life board, and that ministry continues in our community to this day.

The whole premise of both FOCUS and Young Life is to reach out to high school and middle school students by praying with them, building personal relationships with them, and providing fun, life-changing, and skill-building experiences. The foundation of these ministries lies in walking with the young people in friendship that is rooted in Jesus. No matter who the students are, what church they go to, or where they are from, they are welcome.

Personal Application

Take a few moments, either by yourself or in a small group, and reflect on the following questions. You can share your answers with others when you have finished your reflection.

1. When friends of Jesus gather in unity and prayer, powerful things occur in the Holy Spirit. Do you know of others in your area—couples or single individuals—who might like to gather for prayer and fellowship? What is stopping you from making that invitation to them today?

2. Do you have friends and fellow Christians in your life with whom you can share difficulties and celebrate the many joys of friendship with Jesus? If not, how do you hold yourself accountable to the disciplines of prayer, Scripture study, and service to others that characterize friendship with Jesus?

3. What are three issues affecting your local civic community? How might a small group of Christians tackle those issues in the name of Jesus?

CHAPTER 20

Friendship
through the Word

Even though I had twelve years of Catholic education, I never learned that I had a specific role to play in God's plan. It wasn't until I was in my forties that I learned the words that the Lord spoke to the prophet Jeremiah:

> Before I formed you in the womb I knew you,
>> before you were born I dedicated you,
>> a prophet to the nations I appointed you. (1:5)

As I look back, it is clear that I learned much in school *about* Jesus, but I never realized that he was calling me to friendship with him. I am grateful, however, that belief in God and his Church were instilled in me at a young age and grew in me through the years. At no period in my life did I doubt God or his teachings. When I began to study Scripture, however, it was like a veil fell from my eyes, and I began to experience God in a whole new way. I fell passionately in love with Jesus, and I was excited to tell other people about him.

First I went to my pastor and told him what I was experiencing. He blew me off. Basically he told me to stick to the daily readings, and I'd get over it. Needless to say, I was extremely disappointed. (Later he apologized to me, saying that he had not understood me at the time.) Because of this experience, I began to question my religion. If it had not been for the Eucharist, I might have left the Catholic Church. I felt very discouraged and alone.

Then one day, when Nancy and I were in Florida, we heard about a Catholic group called FIRE, which stands for Faith, Intercession, Repentance, and Evangelization. I explored FIRE and found out that they were doing a national rally to be televised at certain locations. Nancy and I went to Boca Raton to visit Florida Atlantic University and attend a closed-circuit program of FIRE.

We sat in the very back of the auditorium. As Ralph Martin, Fr. Mike Scanlan, Fr. John Bertolucci, and Sr. Ann Shields spoke, I started to weep. They confirmed for me that my experience of passionate connection and friendship with Jesus and my new love of Scripture were thoroughly in line with Catholic teaching. This was another day that changed our lives.

I started thinking about my friends. Although many went to church, it had become more of a cultural event for them—as it had been for me for so long. I determined to share with others my friendship with Jesus.

As a result of attending the FIRE program, I started reading Ralph Martin's books. That led Nancy and me into a friendship with Ralph and Peter Herbeck, leaders of Renewal Ministries, which has lasted over thirty years. Ralph and Peter are two of the most Christ-centered, dynamic leaders in the country. Nancy had the privilege of serving for over twenty-five years on the board of Renewal Ministries, and now our son, Michael, is on that board.

One of the greatest gifts I have ever received came from my friend Doug Coe. He promised to teach me everything he knew about Jesus if I promised that each day for the rest of my life I would read something that Jesus taught in the Gospels. So I have studied Scripture every day for thirty-nine years. Doing so has led to a great desire to memorize many passages in the Gospels. I often repeat these passages throughout the day.

By learning the Gospels, I have learned how to evangelize and love. I realized that, as Paul says, "All scripture is inspired by God and is useful for teaching, for refutation, for correction, and for training in righteousness, so that one who belongs to God may be competent, equipped for every good work" (2 Timothy 3:16-17). Nevertheless, the love of Jesus comes through so powerfully in his words, as he moves in his exquisite way through the Gospels.

Getting to Know Jesus

You cannot be a friend of Jesus without knowing him—and if you do not know him, you do not know what he wants of you. However, growing in friendship with Jesus is not difficult because Jesus is not an abstract idea; he is a very real Person. Growing in friendship with him is no different than getting to know another person: we need to spend time with him.

One of the ways we do this is by reading and studying God's word, the Scriptures. In particular, the Gospels teach us to see Jesus as the apostles saw him, to observe how he reacted, to see how he behaved, and to listen to his words. St. Augustine teaches in his commentary on St. John's Gospel that we should read the Gospel as if Jesus were present and speaking to us.

Getting to know Jesus through Scripture helps us move beyond simple facts about him to experience Jesus ourselves. Facts may give us an informative picture about something or someone, but they are no substitute for experience. I may know as a fact that it is often sunny and hot in Florida, for example. However, that knowledge can never substitute for the experience of actually working outside in the sweltering summer heat of Miami. Jesus wants us to experience the freedom that comes with friendship with him, not simply know on an intellectual level that this freedom exists. Therefore Jesus offers all people friendship, which they are free to accept or reject.

Catholics hear Scripture from both the Old and New Testaments at Sunday Mass, with an emphasis on the Gospels. However, unless you know Scripture, you may be hearing a passage read to you out of context. If the priest or deacon doesn't take time to break that Scripture open for you in the homily, you might just receive facts. Facts are only so helpful in establishing a living relationship with Jesus Christ. Knowing the facts about him does not mean that we know him as a friend. Jesus offers friendship to be freely accepted or rejected.

Scripture is very clear about the importance of friendship. The Letter of James tells us, "'Abraham believed God, and it was credited to him as righteousness,' and he was called 'the friend of God'" (2:23, quoting Genesis 15:6; 2 Chronicles 20:7; Isaiah 41:8). In Genesis 5 we hear the story of Enoch, who "walked with God" and was taken bodily to heaven (5:24). The First Letter of John says, "If we walk in the light as he is in the light, then we have fellowship with one another, and the blood of his Son Jesus cleanses us from all sin" (1:7).

When Jesus taught the apostles the Lord's Prayer (the Our Father), he was teaching us how to be friends with the Father:

This is how you are to pray:

Our Father in heaven,
   hallowed be your name,
   your kingdom come,
   your will be done,
      on earth as in heaven.
   Give us today our daily bread;
   and forgive us our debts·
      as we forgive our debtors;
   and do not subject us to the final test,
      but deliver us from the evil one. (Matthew 6:9-13)

Daily reading of Scripture leads us to have an open, sympathetic attitude, which increases our capacity for having friends. Scripture refines the soul through God's grace and helps us understand other people. It also increases our generosity, our optimism, our ability to be positive in social relations, and our gratitude. All these things facilitate friendship for the believer.

Jesus taught us that true friendship is without self-interest, because it consists more in giving than in receiving. It does not seek its own interests but those of the friend. Throughout the centuries, friendship through the Word has been a pathway by which many men and women have come close to Jesus. It is a simple path that eliminates many obstacles and difficulties.

I know that most Christians, especially Catholic Christians, believe in the divinity of Jesus even if they have never really studied Scripture. In my opinion, however, unless you study Scripture, particularly the Gospels, it is impossible to relate to the humanity of Jesus. It is only in relating to the humanity of Jesus that we begin to learn to live as he does—thinking, talking, and acting as he does. And thus we enter into a deep friendship with Jesus as God and Jesus as man.

As I look back over my life, I realize that as a Catholic Christian, I have loved God with all my heart, soul, and strength. But it wasn't until I started reading the Gospels that I began to love God with all my heart, soul, *mind*, and strength. Jesus came so that we could begin to understand God and live in a way pleasing to him. We can now know God through our love for Jesus.

Personal Application

Take a few moments, either by yourself or in a small group, and reflect on the following questions. You can share your answers with others when you have finished your reflection.

1. How comfortable are you with reading the Bible? Would you say that you were encouraged in your life to read Scripture?

2. As you look through the Gospels, what personality traits does Jesus seem to manifest? Have you ever thought about the possibility that, through God's grace, you could possess those same traits? Why or why not?

3. What would it take for you to begin reading the Scriptures, particularly the Gospels, every day? How might you hold yourself accountable for doing so?

CHAPTER 21

Being a Friend

Some time ago, a close business colleague asked me, "Mike, why do you have so many friends? I would like to have friends the way you do, but I don't know how."

That got me thinking about what friendship really is. I realized that to have genuine friendship, you have to be authentic. In other words, what people see is what they get. You have to be totally consistent and not treat people differently depending upon who they are. I also realized that friendship requires availability. With your close friends, you have to be available—even when it's not convenient.

Friendship involves reaching out to others. Scripture says, "Do nothing out of selfishness or out of vainglory; rather, humbly regard others as more important than yourselves, each looking out not for his own interests, but [also] everyone for those of others" (Philippians 2:3-4).

Friendship also means you have to be approachable. Your personality either attracts or repels people. One of the most important aspects of approachability is eye contact with others and smiling at them, so that you present a welcoming spirit.

Sharing authentic friendship with others is an essential form of evangelization. In this context, evangelization means simply sharing with someone our relationship with Jesus—cultivated through prayer and meditation on Holy Scripture. People are not objects of ministry, however. Christian friendship must be sincere and authentic, not a strategic activity or a tool to lure people into a commitment to Jesus.

In fact, authentic Christian friendship should be an end in itself—something we pursue because we genuinely love other people and not because we possess any ulterior motive. Because we love others, we genuinely want them to experience goodness. Thus, to introduce (or reintroduce) Jesus Christ to another person is the greatest good of human friendship.

Making New Friends

One day, after I had committed everything to Jesus, I was in a fruit market putting a number of oranges in a bag. A woman on the other side of the display, an acquaintance of mine, was doing the same thing. She looked at me and said, "Why are you so different? What has happened to you? You are so open, friendly, and peaceful."

I decided to tell her what had happened to me. It was one of the first times I had shared my testimony. As I was talking to her, at least a dozen people gathered around us in the fruit market, just listening to me. The next week this woman's husband joined my Bible study.

This experience taught me a great lesson: all of us are seeking people to whom we can relate as friends. We have a hunger for friendship, whether we know it or not. That hunger can be completely satisfied only by coming to know Jesus, who is the ultimate friend.

Friendship is a risk. It requires us to open our hearts and minds without fear of rejection and to be kind and forgiving. It does not provide immunity from being hurt or even betrayed. I have endured both those experiences, and they were extremely painful. However, that pain did not deter me from meeting the good friends that I have, nor did it dull my desire to continue to make new friends.

Jesus wants us to spread "the odor of the knowledge of him in every place. For we are the aroma of Christ for God among those who are being saved" (2 Corinthians 2:14-15).

Many times on airplanes, people have seen me reading the Bible and then asked me questions. Inevitably, they were seekers. One of the most dramatic occurrences of this was when I was traveling home from Washington after extensive meetings with Doug Coe. I was exhausted. I planned to read my Bible and then fall asleep.

We had not yet taken off, and the man sitting next to me had a martini. After we took off, he drank another martini. I was quietly reading, and he asked me, "Are you reading the Bible?"

I said, "Yes."

He asked, "Do you always read it?"

I replied, "Yes, every day."

He then said that he was married with two kids, and he felt as if he had the perfect life. He told me how much money he made. All of this came without any prompting from me.

I said to him, "I think it's wonderful that you have a perfect life," and I continued reading.

About five minutes later, he asked me another question: "What would you do if your daughter told your wife to 'go F herself' this morning?"

I quickly responded, "I thought you told me you had a perfect life."

"My life is a disaster," he replied.

I pointed out that he probably drank too much, and I asked him if I could tell him about a friend of mine named Jesus. So I shared my testimony with him. When we landed in Detroit, he said he had a long layover, so he decided to walk with me to my car. As we navigated the airport maze, I explained that he was at a crossroads in life and God was reaching out to him through me.

I also said that he had a choice to make. He could ask Jesus to become Lord of his life or not. But if he did not, he was headed for divorce and misery. So leaning on the hood of my car, he prayed to receive Jesus. I told him who he could contact in the city where he lived, to continue growing in the Lord.

My point in telling this story is to highlight the fact that my selfishness in not wanting to be available to anyone on that flight home did not inhibit the Lord. Jesus had another plan. He wanted me to be a friend to someone whom he loved and for whom he died.

An Unlikely Friend

In an effort to deepen our understanding of the wider body of Christ, Nancy and I decided to go to a large charismatic conference at the Superdome in New Orleans. After we checked into the hotel, we left for the conference in a cab. The driver was an African American and a veteran of the war in Vietnam. Truth be told, he appeared to be a very angry man.

As we approached the stadium, this driver said he knew this was a Christian conference because of the signage. "I think it is good for you white people," he said. "I understand why you white people go to a Christian conference, but it makes me furious to see black people coming as well. They have no reason to be with you."

I asked him whether he thought Jesus loved only white people. He didn't answer, though I pressed on. Finally we arrived at the Superdome, and Nancy and I got out of the cab. I thanked him for listening to me, and we went to the conference.

When we came out of the conference, providentially, we got into the same cab, with the same driver who had driven us there. We picked up our discussion about Jesus where we had left off. The driver took us back to the hotel, and I said that if he wanted to pick us up tomorrow, I would give him a big tip.

He said, "OK."

And once again he drove us to the conference. He listened to me speak about Jesus, and I tried to answer his questions. He was a very lonely, dispirited man who suffered deeply from his experiences as a veteran of a tragic war.

Once again the man was there when we came out of the conference, and he drove us back to our hotel. I told him we were leaving New Orleans the next day, and I asked if he would like to take us to the airport. He said yes.

On the way to the airport, we talked more about Jesus, and the man began to weep. When we arrived at the departure section of the airport, he stopped the cab. He was sobbing uncontrollably. We got out of the cab, and then he got out of the cab. We stood together, and he asked me to lead him to Jesus.

The principle behind this story is that sometimes the friend that Jesus wants you to make is a person that you would not notice. Sometimes he sends friends into your life unexpectedly.

Making Connections with Friends of Friends

About fifteen years ago, Nancy and I hosted a reception at our home in Naples, Florida, on behalf of Prison Fellowship US. Chuck Colson told me he had invited two men to the reception. "I think these men will become two of your best friends," he said. While I deeply respected Chuck, I thought the likelihood of that happening was slim.

Their names were Hal Rosser and Matt Evans. At that time, both lived in Connecticut and spent time in Florida during the winter. Little did I know that both men would indeed become two of my closest friends. In the years that followed, Matt was one of several men who would meet with me to study Scripture.

Hal Rosser accompanied me and Ed Russell on a vision trip to visit prisons in Belize and Costa Rica in 2009. Anytime you take a trip with someone, you really get to know them. It was on that trip that Hal explained to us the purpose of the New Canaan Society, the ecumenical men's group that I detailed in chapter 16. Hal and his wife, Rita, went to Africa twice with Nancy and me, visiting our schools and homes.

These friendships continue to this day, as all three of us couples meet every week with two additional couples to discuss some point about Jesus from Scripture. We three men are all active in leadership positions in the New Canaan Society as well.

Friends in Ministry

One of the most important gifts a person can receive is a friend who is an encourager—who listens, laughs, and prays with you. God gave me such a friend when I joined the Board of Prison Fellowship in 1990. Dallen Peterson comes to my house almost every day around 5:00 p.m. for a drink, and we share the day's experiences. When this is not possible, Dallen and I talk on the phone almost every day. He is the type of friend who keeps me grounded in the ways of the Lord.

All the examples of friendship that I have given in this chapter flow from this reality: to be open to friendship, you have to be approachable, available, and accountable. Many years ago, a close friend said to me, "Mike, you have become very public in your belief and love for Jesus. If you personally fail, you will take many people with you."

I have never forgotten that caveat. And therefore I try to live a Jesus-centered life.

Personal Application

Take a few moments, either by yourself or in a small group, and reflect on the following questions. You can share your answers with others when you have finished your reflection.

1. Do you find it easy to remain approachable in social situations? Why or why not?

2. What do you think it means to make yourself available for friendships in your life? What might that availability look like?

3. How does Jesus make himself available to us as a friend? In what ways can we spend time with him?

4. What does Jesus' availability tell us about what God might be asking of us in terms of our availability to others?

CHAPTER 22

Helping Friends around the World

As my commitment to Jesus grew, I had a growing desire to use the wealth that God had allowed us to achieve to help others.

In February of 1986, I was invited to the National Prayer Breakfast in Washington, DC. I went with Dick Robarts from Canada; he had mentored me and introduced me to Doug Coe. I really didn't understand what the breakfast was all about, but I was astounded to see people from every background imaginable—Christian and non-Christian, from over 150 countries.

While waiting for some friends in an area where tea and coffee were served, I witnessed something remarkable. A European woman, an African man, and an Asian man sat around a small table. They were holding hands as they prayed with their heads bowed. It was the first time I really understood the words "God so loved the world that he gave his only Son" (John 3:16). That moment would change my outlook for the rest of my life.

Because of this Washington connection, I started attending retreats at which I met people from all over the world. At a retreat in the mountains of Colorado, Nancy and I met a group of Peruvians, and we became instant friends. They invited us to come to Peru, explaining that the country was in deep political turmoil. The *Sendero Luminoso* (a Maoist terrorist organization committed to overthrowing the government of Peru) was trying to destroy the country through insurrection, causing extreme poverty. Inspired by these friends, we visited Peru at least twice a year for twelve years. We did some projects for the poor: building schools and markets and developing other initiatives.

One of the most meaningful projects we undertook involved children with Down syndrome. We discovered that many poor families who had children with Down syndrome kept them at home all the time. These children were not allowed to be seen, and they were often chained to their beds. Many of these parents believed that their child's condition was a direct result of a sin they themselves had committed. They were ashamed.

We decided to construct a very special building in one of the poorest areas of Lima. Now, it has not rained in Lima for over fifty years, so many of the poor live in cardboard houses. Nothing green grows in these poor areas, and the dust is constant. In contrast to these conditions, we painted our building stark white and placed a little plot of grass and a tree on either side of the front door.

Through our Peruvian friends, we arranged for a doctor and nurses to volunteer on a daily basis. We put the word out that this building was for the special children: only Down syndrome children could come to this special place. Little did I know that, twenty years later, God would bless us with a Down syndrome grandson, who is the light of our family.

The friends we made in Peru taught us so much about becoming friends with the poor. We started doing similar work in the mountains of Honduras, in a place called Zacapa. Tom Monaghan, the founder of Domino's Pizza and a good friend, invited my son and me to go to Honduras and see the work that he had started there. Because Domino's had run into some financial problems, Tom hoped that we would carry on some of his work in the area.

We met a priest named Fr. Enrique Silvestre, who served the very poor. His parish had over fifty thousand people in it—almost all of them destitute. He wanted to help them not only materially but also spiritually. He was training young people to become catechists who could go to the outlying villages in the mountains and share the good news of Jesus Christ.

In much of Latin America, people are born Catholic and die Catholic, but they don't have much experience living their Catholic faith in between. We had this great desire to evangelize the poor, but we realized that words are empty when you are desperately hungry and can barely survive. So we determined that we would do projects for the poor, such as teaching them how to farm, how to can food, and so on. After more than a year of helping them, we started to share the gospel with them, so that they would understand that Jesus loves them and wants to be their friend.

As we worked in Peru and Honduras, we became good friends with many of the people we served. Often, when my wife and I visited our projects with the poor, we had to travel in cars with blacked-out windows. We would put our friends in danger if certain people knew that "gringos" were behind a project.

It has always been our practice to share and show the love of Jesus through friendship before we talk about having a friendship with him. Unless you experience the love of Jesus, it is difficult to understand who he is. A Scripture passage that has been extremely important to us is from the Letter of James: "What good is it, my brothers, if someone says he has faith but does not have works? Can that faith save him? . . . So also faith of itself, if it does not have works, is dead" (2:14, 17). To the poor, one of the most powerful ways you can really demonstrate friendship is by helping them concretely.

Helping at Home

Around the time our projects in Honduras and Peru were taking off, a man came to me and said, "I understand that you are helping many people around the world. Whom are you helping in your city?"

At that time, we were supporting many causes in our city, but we were not personally involved with the poor. Then I became friends with an African American pastor, Eddie Edwards, who had started a mission called Joy of Jesus. He wanted to change a huge part of the lower east side of Detroit and make it into a beautiful neighborhood where young people could live without fear and where there would be a real sense of community centered around the person of Jesus.

Eddie and I became great friends, and I was able to help him by giving and raising support so that he could buy defunct buildings and renew them, as well as repair homes. This went on for many years until his unfortunate death. I know that many young people were saved through Eddie's efforts.

We were also concerned about the education of young people in Detroit, as the educational system there was sadly lacking. Many non-Catholic parents wanted to send their children to parochial schools in Detroit, but they did not have the finances to do so. I gathered a group of friends together, and we formed a foundation called Pathways of Hope. Pathways provided parochial school scholarships to young non-Catholic, African American students. In addition, through the efforts of Cardinal Adam Maida, a group of friends formed Cornerstone school, which provided the African American community Christ-centered educational excellence. The school rapidly expanded but eventually became a charter school.

All these efforts were accomplished in Jesus through the bonds of friendship we formed with others.

Personal Application

Take a few moments, either by yourself or in a small group, and reflect on the following questions. You can share your answers with others when you have finished your reflection.

1. This chapter points out that often people must experience the love of God in concrete acts of service before they can open their hearts to friendship with him. Can you remember a time in your life when you felt the love of God personally through the actions, service, or attention of someone? What happened? How did it affect your attitude, stance, or belief in God?

2. Have you given thought to the deep needs of the men and women stricken by poverty in your local community? Besides donating money, what are some ways you might serve the poor while building friendships with them?

CHAPTER 23

Unusual Friends

Over the years, God has allowed me to meet many unusual people. Without the grace of Jesus, I might never have experienced the blessings of these friendships.

Some years ago, a friend asked me to go with him to a Michigan prison to meet an inmate he had been walking with for quite some time. For the sake of confidentiality, I will call the prisoner Joe. Joe was serving a twenty-year sentence for carrying a certain amount of marijuana as a "mule" from Texas to Michigan. At that time, Michigan law dictated that if you were found guilty of carrying a certain amount of narcotics, you received a twenty-year, no-parole sentence. Joe was in the eleventh year of his sentence, and he had become a strong believer in Jesus during his incarceration.

After meeting with Joe a few times, I decided to approach the governor of Michigan, whom I knew as a friend. I told him about this prisoner and said that it did not make any sense for a nonviolent offender to serve twenty years. I demonstrated to the governor how much this man's incarceration cost the state, and then I asked him for a pardon. I told the governor

I would take Joe into my home, provide him with a job, and mentor him. I had previously done a big favor for the governor, and I felt that I was not asking for much.

The governor was approaching the end of his term in office when I asked him, and I received no immediate reply. However, a couple of weeks before he was to leave office, his attorney called me and said, "Mike, you lost the battle and won the war." I asked her what that meant, and she said that the governor felt I was correct about the mandatory "twenty years with no parole" issue, and he had asked the legislature to change the law. She said, "Therefore the prisoner that you interceded for will be eligible for parole in a very short time."

Three months later, Joe was released. We took him into our home, and he worked on our landscaping, did odd jobs, painted, and so on. He worked forty hours per week with pay. We helped him buy a truck.

Eleven years of prison had taken a huge toll on Joe's ability to make decisions. He was very unsure of himself. Nancy mentored him, which really helped. A group of my friends also came around him and had fellowship with him. He even joined a local community church.

We suggested that Joe take a course to become a home inspector, because that did not require a license from the state, something that convicted felons had difficulty acquiring. Joe took the course and received the certificate. After two years with us, he moved to mid-Michigan and established a business. Today he is an assistant pastor at a small community church and a married man.

Helping Joe opened my eyes to the tremendous difficulties involved in the rehabilitation of prisoners. Many are released without any help or guidance, and consequently, they return to a life of crime in order to survive. This is why programs like Prison Fellowship, Prison Alpha, and the Salvation Army are so important. They reach out to those who are least, last, and lost to help them lead normal lives.

Years ago Doug Coe called me and suggested that I would learn a lot if I took a man into my office and discipled him for a two-year period. This was at a time when I was working ten to twelve hours per day. Needless to say, I was reluctant. If anyone but Doug had asked me to do that, I would have refused. But I agreed.

John Moolenaar, a man in his late twenties, came to Detroit to see me. Every day he would sit at a table in the corner of my office as I went about my daily duties. I asked some dear friends if he could live with them, because they had the space. In an act of great generosity, they made him part of their family.

The first year John was with me was very difficult for me. I came to the conclusion that I should ask him to leave. However, I felt Jesus telling me to persevere and make our relationship work. And it did. Following his time with me, John went into local politics, married, and had children. He was elected to both the House and the Senate in the state of Michigan. He then ran for a seat in the United States Congress for Michigan's Fourth District; he has now been elected three times to that position.

John is a very special legislator. Ever since he entered politics, he has been a reconciler. He is a great example of a man possessing strong Jesus-centered values as a public official, while not alienating himself from people who disagree with his views. Consequently, this Republican has made many friends across the aisle. He and his close friend Tom Suozzi, a Democratic Congressman from New York, have been cochairs of the National Prayer Breakfast in Washington for the last two years. John is the best example I know of friendship through reconciliation.

Personal Application

Take a few moments, either by yourself or in a small group, and reflect on the following questions. You can share your answers with others when you have finished your reflection.

1. Sometimes unusual situations require an unusual level of response. Both John Moolenaar and Joe were taken in to live with families and were rehabilitated and healed through deep hospitality, community, and friendship. Has there ever been a time in your life when you have responded to the needs of another person with exceptional generosity or hospitality?

2. What do you think stops people from responding generously to persons and situations?

3. What could you do to free yourself up to be radically available to those in need, responding with a deep generosity to their unique situations? What is holding you back from living that life of generous friendship with others?

CHAPTER 24

Using Friendship with Jesus to Reach Others

Over the last two years, there have been extensive articles in both *The Wall Street Journal* and *The New York Times* on the loneliness of the American man. The reports say that there is a culture of loneliness among men who pretend that they are not lonely. American men can be extremely careful about offering and accepting friendship because seeking real and lasting friendship opens up a minefield of cultural prohibitions—such as homophobia, fear of rejection, and shaming. It has been empirically proven that lonely men have higher rates of violence, drug abuse, unemployment, alcoholism, divorce, and suicide. Sociologists state that the biggest threat facing middle-aged men is not a health issue per se; it is loneliness.

Despite the fact that men need real relationships with other men, they shy away from them. Emotional connection is often thought of as a female trait. From an early age, we are taught to "man up," push our emotions down, and stoically endure whenever we have a difficult problem rather than deal with it. Men struggle to express deep feelings with others, preferring to talk about sports and work rather than reveal their personal feelings. As men, they tend to experience isolation because of the demands of family, life, work, and the rapacious drive for material success.

Cigna, a global health service company, did a recent survey of twenty thousand Americans using the UCLA Loneliness Scale. The study found that adults aged eighteen to twenty-five are the loneliest segment of the population. Nearly 50 percent report a chronic sense of loneliness. Real friendship is the only cure for the loneliness that so many young people feel. They will not find real friendship on a smartphone or computer but only through the lasting bond of true personal friendship.

The loneliness of men was brought home to me by a recent email I received from an acquaintance. I had met this man perhaps four or five times before, and always in a group. The email was a plea for me to talk to him because he was feeling despondent over the constraints imposed by the COVID-19 pandemic lockdown. He was bickering with his wife and children, and he felt he had no one to talk to.

Needless to say, I called this man, and we talked for an hour. He said that he did not have any friends to whom he could explain how he felt. I felt sad for him; I also realized that he was a typical American male. The good news is that the next day, he emailed to tell me that our talk had helped him reconcile with his wife and see things differently.

Loneliness Close to Home

My father had no close male friends. I, the youngest of five, never had a substantive conversation with him about anything except sports, until he was in his late 80s. Then we started talking about the Gospels.

My two brothers, although they loved each other, were not particularly close. And neither of them had many, if any, close male friends. Yet they both interacted lovingly with their many children.

While I write this from the standpoint of a man, many of these points are equally applicable to women. I know that many women feel lonely and isolated, particularly when they have lost their husbands through divorce or death or do not communicate well with their spouses. We are losing the art of friendship even in our homes.

To make the problem worse, we are certainly not passing it on to our children. Young children are given smart-phones, computers, Xboxes, and so on, which lead to isolation and the inability to socialize. Before COVID struck, it was very common to go to a restaurant and observe a husband, wife, and children sitting around the table looking at their smart-phones and only occasionally talking to one another. If you are unable to socialize, you become incapable of friendship.

All of this points to the need and deep desire of men and women to have significant friends with whom they can share their lives, their problems, and their joys.

Nicky Gumbel, in a recent reference from his "Bible in One Year," pointed out a survey done with millennials (those born between 1981 and 1996):

The results portrayed an alarming picture of an increasingly lonely and lost generation. . . . On average, Millennials spend six-and-a-half hours a day on social media. . . . [The survey] found people had a very large number of "friends" but an increasing sense of loneliness.[5]

The point is that social media is no substitute for real face-to-face friendships. We were created for friendship with God and with each other.

This loneliness and our ingrained need for socialization present a tremendous opportunity for the Church and believers. We often hear young people talk about someone being their "bff" (best friend forever). Even if it is a bit of a cliché, the truth is that Jesus does want to be our best friend forever. Therefore we can approach others from that perspective!

What's in a Name?

In the preceding chapters, I have tried to point out how reaching out to others, no matter where they stand in relationship with Jesus, has enabled me to connect others with Jesus. One of the problems in the church, and particularly in the Catholic Church, is that we seem reluctant to use the name of Jesus. We will use the terms "God," "Lord," and "Christ" regularly but the name of Jesus very sparingly. I have heard many homilies in which the name "Jesus" was not even mentioned. I asked a bishop once why we do not use the name of Jesus more. He said, "Mike, I think it is because we are embarrassed to use his name."

I am incredibly thankful to my Protestant Evangelical friends who never hesitate to use the name of Jesus. The interesting thing is that there is a supernatural transaction of grace when we use the name "Jesus." Philippians 2:10-11 tells us

> that at the name of Jesus
> every knee should bend,
> of those in heaven and on earth and under the earth,
> and every tongue confess that
> Jesus Christ is Lord,
> to the glory of God the Father.

I use this personal example: If someone is talking about me and uses my last name, Timmis, it does not particularly indicate familiarity. But if they use my first name, Mike, people tend to assume that we are friends. It always amazes me how often Christians, particularly Catholic Christians, do not use the name of Jesus. They usually say "Christ," which is not the last name of Jesus but rather his title as the Messiah or Anointed One of God.

St. Josemaría Escrivá, in his book *The Way*, advises us, "Don't be afraid to call our Lord by His name—Jesus—and to tell him that you love him."[6] The point is that we call our friends by their first names. So why are we reluctant to call our greatest friend by his first name?

The Father gave Jesus his name through the message of an angel, before he was conceived in Mary's womb (see Luke 1:31). The name "Jesus" means "he who saves" or "our Savior who has brought us salvation." The Jews attached great importance to names because the name given to someone represented what that person would be in the future.

We see this in the passage concerning the birth of John the Baptist. The friends of Zechariah and Elizabeth did not accept the name "John" for their friends' baby, until Zechariah, who could not speak at that point, wrote, "John is his name" (Luke 1:63). Zechariah could then speak, and he glorified God.

In fulfillment of the sign of the covenant that God had made with the Jewish people, Jesus was circumcised on the eighth day. That is when he officially received his name, Jesus (see Luke 2:21).

On a personal note, I have traveled to over 120 countries to meet with leaders and with prisoners. In talking about Jesus and using his name, I have never had any pushback. There is a supernatural outpouring of grace when we use the name "Jesus." Even in countries like Iraq, Syria, Yemen, and Russia, I have never had an argument when talking about Jesus.

Chapter 17 of John's Gospel demonstrates to me the incredible power in the name of Jesus. When we reach out to others in Jesus' name, we make his love and friendship present to them.

Jesus' Friends

The great commandment is that I love God with my heart, soul, mind, and strength. Then I must love my neighbor as myself. When I recite these together, I realize that through the love of God, I can love my neighbor as a friend, and I can grow in my friendship with Jesus at the same time.

There is no simple formula for reaching out in friendship with Jesus to others. However, if we examine the life of Jesus, we can see how the Master prioritized friendship. There is no report of him from the time he was twelve and found in the Temple until he was thirty and started his public ministry. Obviously, Jesus did not live in a bubble. He was like us in all things but sin, and he probably knew many people. Many people also knew him and were attracted to him. Scripture tells us his approach in choosing the twelve apostles:

> In those days he departed to the mountain to pray, and he spent the night in prayer to God. When day came, he called his disciples to himself, and from them he chose Twelve, whom he also named apostles: Simon, whom he named Peter, and his brother Andrew, James, John, Philip, Bartholomew, Matthew, Thomas, James the son of Alphaeus, Simon who was called a Zealot, and Judas the son of James, and Judas Iscariot, who became a traitor. (Luke 6:12-16)

Jesus prayed to the Father throughout the night. When he came down from the mountain, a group of his friends awaited him. It was then he chose the Twelve.

There had to be great camaraderie and friendship among these young men, or they would not have followed Jesus. It was only gradually that they began to recognize him as the Messiah. Right from the beginning, he made it clear that he was calling the disciples and us as heirs. We would not be his servants but his friends (see John 15:12-15).

After Pentecost, the Church grew rapidly. It is very clear that friendship was key.

> They devoted themselves to the teaching of the apostles and to the communal life, to the breaking of the bread and to the

prayers. Awe came upon everyone, and many wonders and signs were done through the apostles. All who believed were together and had all things in common; they would sell their property and possessions and divide them among all according to each one's need. Every day they devoted themselves to meeting together in the temple area and to breaking bread in their homes. They ate their meals with exultation and sincerity of heart, praising God and enjoying favor with all the people. And every day the Lord added to their number those who were being saved. (Acts 2:42-47)

The early followers shared community, fellowship, their lives, and their goods with one another. Friendship was the hallmark of the early Church. As that friendship spread from one person to another, the story of Jesus spread across the Middle East and beyond. Within seventy-five years of the Resurrection, Christian churches existed in major cities throughout the Roman Empire. There were tens of thousands of Christian families from all social classes—from slaves all the way up to members of the imperial household.

This growth continued for another two hundred years, all under the banner of the Roman empire, with intermittent and bloody persecutions. There were certainly no civil or social advantages to being a Christian. Yet by 313, while claiming the allegiance of only 10 percent of the population of the Roman Empire, the infant Church won tolerance with the Edict of Milan. Within another seventy-five years, Christianity became the official Church of Rome. Beginning at that time, Christian morals were gradually introduced into the law of the empire.

The growth of Christianity in those first centuries was due to the prayer, moral behavior, and charitable works of the followers of Jesus. These men and women communicated their love of Jesus and his Church to the people around them through friendship. Without that friendship, the Church would not have survived.

On Being Born Again

I was speaking to a group of men a few years ago, and for the first time, I emphasized what I had learned about friendship from the Scriptures. I called upon the men to consider becoming a friend of Jesus. As I was leaving the event, a man came rushing up to me and asked, "Is this what it is all about? Becoming friends with Jesus?"

I said, "Yes, of course."

He replied that he had heard religious terms like "being born again" for fifteen years, and he never really understood what they meant. Unfortunately, many have taken one passage from Scripture—Jesus' visit with Nicodemus in John 3—and made it a litmus test when speaking to others about committing their lives to Jesus. It is quite common for someone to ask, "Are you born again?" In my experience, the person asking often does not understand what he has just asked.

Jesus explained what "born again" means in John 3:16: "God so loved the world that he gave his only Son, so that everyone who believes in him might not perish but might have eternal life."

John wrote in his first letter, "And this is the testimony: God gave us eternal life, and this life is in his Son. Whoever possesses the Son has life; whoever does not possess the Son of God does not have life" (5:11-12). And the apostle Paul makes it totally clear:

> [I]f you confess with your mouth that Jesus is Lord and believe in your heart that God raised him from the dead, you will be saved. For one believes with the heart and so is justified, and one confesses with the mouth and so is saved. (Romans 10:9-10)

Furthermore, Paul says, "No one who believes in him will be put to shame" (Romans 10:11). And in Acts 16:31, Paul and Silas said, "Believe in the Lord Jesus and you and your household will be saved."

The point here is that there are numerous passages about being saved, and they are all grounded in belief in Jesus, which includes a surrender of one's life and repentance. This surrender and repentance aren't simply isolated or final moments in the journey of salvation. In the Book of Acts, Peter gives this command: "Repent and be baptized, every one of you, in the name of Jesus Christ for the forgiveness of your sins; and you will receive the gift of the holy Spirit" (2:38). In the story of Jesus' meeting with Nicodemus, Jesus is clear that Baptism is a necessary component of the process of being born again (the process of salvation): "Amen, amen, I say to you, no one can enter the kingdom of God without being born of water and Spirit" (John 3:5).

In Baptism we receive the very life of Jesus through the power of the Holy Spirit and are regenerated. In this way, we fulfill the passage from 1 John 5 quoted earlier: we possess the Son and so receive life. And I believe that is a process that goes on from the moment of our Baptism until the day we die and join him. Every day brings with it the possibility of cooperating with the life of Jesus, surrendering to him, and growing in friendship with him.

A year and a half ago, I was speaking to a group of men in northern Florida about friendship with Jesus. A man came up to me after the event and said, "I was born again forty years ago, but I would never consider Jesus my friend."

This statement reflects a huge problem among many Christians today. They want to worship the divine, and they believe that Jesus lived and died for them; but they have no relationship with Jesus in his humanity. For them Jesus is eternally transcendent, above and beyond them. They miss the reality that Jesus is also Emmanuel, "God with us," LIVING in the midst of human joy and suffering. Without knowing Jesus in this way, it is impossible to think, talk, or act like him.

Holiness and Friendship with Jesus

As I discussed earlier, many people no longer feel obliged to go to church. Attendance, particularly after the COVID-19 pandemic lockdown, is at an all-time low. In addition, I never cease to be amazed at how few people practice a daily discipline of prayer and Scripture reading. Without that daily discipline, it is impossible to evangelize others, much less yourself.

Those who do have a daily discipline become like people magnets because people are drawn to holiness, and holiness, as Scripture says, is Jesus in you. "It is due to him that you are in Christ Jesus, who became for us wisdom from him, as well as righteousness, sanctification, and redemption" (1 Corinthians 1:30).

Once Jesus is in you, you express him to others in your daily existence. To introduce (or reintroduce) a person to Jesus is the greatest good of human friendship.

Friendship in Scripture

Scripture is very clear on the importance of friendship, especially in the Book of Sirach:

> Faithful friends are a sturdy shelter;
>   whoever finds one finds a treasure.
> Faithful friends are beyond price,
>   no amount can balance their worth.
> Faithful friends are life-saving medicine;
>   those who fear God will find them.
> Those who fear the Lord enjoy stable friendship,
>   for as they are, so will their neighbors be. (6:14-19)

The Great Commandment is basically a commandment on friendship. By loving God with my heart, soul, strength, and mind, I love him as my best friend. Loving my neighbor as myself really means loving others for the love of Christ and being their friend for the sake of my friendship with Christ.

Unfortunately, we don't communicate that often. We see Jesus state it clearly, though, in the Gospel of John:

> No one has greater love than this, to lay down one's life for one's friends. You are my friends if you do what I command you. I

no longer call you slaves, because a slave does not know what his master is doing. I have called you friends, because I have told you everything I have heard from my Father. (15:13–15)

It is absolutely clear that Jesus came to connect us with his humanity, and this is evidenced in the apostles. They became great friends with Jesus because he loved them, spent time with them, and lived with them. Eventually, they understood his words, "I give you a new commandment: love one another. As I have loved you, so you also should love one another" (John 13:34).

Jesus sought and encouraged friendship with everyone he met. As you read the Gospels, you can witness how Jesus made conversation in order to make a connection with people—like Martha, Mary, Lazarus, Zacchaeus, as well as the apostles. For example, Jesus showed the depth of his friendship as he wept over the death of his friend Lazarus (see John 11:33-36). Even as Jesus' death was unfolding, he referred to Judas as his friend, as he had called the other eleven disciples a few hours before, at the Last Supper (see Matthew 26:50; John 15:15).

Jesus is a friend who is always with us, and while we see him mostly in the shadows of life, he fills our whole life. He wants us to know he is with us constantly. He wants us to constantly acknowledge him as we go through life. The more we talk to him, the more he encourages us.

When I started traveling around the world witnessing to leaders, I initially felt fear related to the possibility of rejection. I remember Doug Coe telling me, "Mike, don't forget that Jesus and you are a majority." As I pondered that, my fear vanished.

Friendship with Jesus grows as we get to know him better and better, especially through our encounters with him in the Gospels and the rest of the New Testament. Friendship with Jesus helps me understand the essence of friendship and therefore how to be a better friend. And there is nothing so precious as a faithful friend.

Friendship and the Apostles

The apostles were a disparate group when you think about it. Matthew was a tax collector, Simon a Zealot, and others were fishermen. It was only through Jesus' friendship that they were able to unite and indeed become friends with one another.

We see great examples of friendship in the various epistles of Paul, which could actually be called the epistles of Paul and his friends. In 1 Corinthians, it's Paul and Sosthenes writing. In 2 Corinthians, it's Paul and Timothy. In Thessalonians, it's Paul, Silvanus, and Timothy. The point is that Paul was not evangelizing by himself. He was usually advancing the cause of Christ with friends. Throughout his travels, it was he and his friends who explained why Jesus had come and passed on what he taught.

This is important to understand because it provides a template for us in advancing the cause of Jesus. C. S. Lewis pointed out, "To the Ancients, Friendship seemed the happiest and most fully human of all loves; / the crown of life and the school of virtue."[7]

Friendship and the Diversity of Gifts

As we were leaving Mother Teresa at the end of our first visit with her in 1989, she said, "I do what you cannot do. But you do what I cannot do. And together we can do something beautiful for God." That's why it is so important to have good friends united together in friendship with Jesus today.

I believe the reason Jesus sent out his disciples two by two was that ministry can be very lonely, and friendships make all the difference. It doesn't mean, however, that friendships are always easy. In chapter 15 of the Book of Acts, we see how Paul and Barnabas parted in sharp disagreement and went their separate ways. However, in the end it worked out. Mark became Barnabas' new friend in ministry, and Paul found a great friend in Silas as he went through Syria and Cilicia.

Sometimes friendships struggle and even fail. Only Jesus can bring reconciliation in those situations—because Jesus always calls us to forgiveness. The greater our friendship with Jesus, the greater our capacity for having friends. As we pray to Jesus, our prayer helps us understand and accept other people and avoid feeling superior or judgmental.

Friendship increases social relationships as well as gratitude. Friendship also consists more in giving than in receiving, and it looks out for the interests of the other. However, true friendship requires mutuality. If that is present, the friendship will grow in strength when there are difficulties.

As a friend suffers, we suffer, because a good friend does not turn away when problems arise. A real friend also never speaks badly of the other and never allows his friends to be demeaned. When Nancy and I lost our daughter, Laura, we learned what true friendship was. Our friends in Jesus grieved with us, prayed for us, supported us, and comforted us.

Friendship and the Spread of the Gospel

Friendship in Jesus spread throughout the Middle East and then to Europe and the world, as friends shared the teachings of Jesus with others. This still occurs today. In the course of writing this book, a friend in Argentina, Bill Murchison, whom I met at a meeting in Lima, Peru, in 1990, invited me to participate in a Zoom call.

Bill convenes a group of men from different countries in Latin America whom I have met through my travels. For decades they have shared a monthly call to talk about Jesus and their lives. Through their efforts, many wonderful things have happened in Latin America in regard to evangelization, the establishment of businesses, and groups forming in the name of Jesus, as well as work for the poor. This demonstrates so well how friendship in Jesus endures over time and distance, just as it did in the Acts of the Apostles and thereafter.

The greatest gift I can give a friend is another friend. The first time Nancy and I went to East Africa with our son and nephew, a Christian group asked me to speak to a group of parliamentarians about my journey to Jesus. While we were in Kenya, I met a man who was the head of Fiat East Africa. He invited our family to their home for dinner. At dinner he said, "I understand that you have been meeting with leaders about Jesus."

I confirmed that, and he asked me what denomination I was. When I told him that I was a Roman Catholic, he seemed quite surprised. He was also Catholic, and he said he had never heard of any Catholic businessman talking to groups about Jesus. After dinner we retreated into his library, and I shared my testimony with him. It went on so long that we almost missed our midnight flight to Europe!

A couple of years later, my secretary informed me that there was a man in our reception area who wanted to see me. He had told her that he met me in Africa two years before. He came into my office, and we had a nice chat. He had left Kenya and moved to Grosse Pointe, and he had bought a house only a mile from ours. I told him that I would like to introduce him to a number of really fine men. Every Wednesday evening I teach a Bible study to a lot of men like him.

This man initially said no to my invitation, indicating that the Bible study just wasn't for him. Then he said his goodbyes and left. A half hour later, he was back in my office; he had decided to accept my invitation. He was an active participant for many years.

At a certain point, however, this man wrote me a letter saying how disappointed he was that I did not have more time for him as a friend. In those days, I worked ten to twelve hours a day and taught two Scripture groups. I literally had no time for myself. What he did not realize is that I knew this was a problem before he mentioned it to me. Therefore I had asked my best friend to become friends with him, because I knew he wanted a deeper friendship, but I could not invest the time. My best friend said yes and began to walk with this man as a friend.

Once I informed this Kenyan what I had done, he realized the situation, and our friendship increased. A few years later, he went home to be with the Lord. I knew I had given him the greatest gift that I could give: the gift of another friend. Of course, the greatest gift of all is to give someone the friendship of Jesus.

As I have said, I have always believed that the greater my friendship with Jesus, the more I can cooperate with his grace and presence within me. While this journey is an inward one, it impacts the world greatly. For the deeper I go, the more Jesus can use me to share friendship with others. If I do not act as a friend, I am not acting like Jesus but rather using some methodology or words of proselytizing that ultimately accomplish nothing.

The older I become, the more clearly I recognize the Father's plan simply as Jesus embodied it in the Great Commandment. When we love the Lord our God with all our heart, soul, strength, and mind, we become more and more like him. We accept ourselves as he sees, accepts, and loves us. It is through this love that we can truly reach out in friendship to our neighbors and love them as ourselves.

Personal Application

Take a few moments, either by yourself or in a small group, and reflect on the following questions. You can share your answers with others when you have finished your reflection.

1. As this chapter points out, the apostles were not alone in their missionary activity. They gathered friends around them who assisted them. If you were going to spend some time trying to serve a group of people and introduce them to Jesus, which of your friends would you bring along, and why?

2. Not everyone can do everything perfectly. We all have different strengths, talents, and spiritual gifts. What are three strengths that you would bring to serving others and helping them become friends with Jesus?

3. Have you ever been able to gift a friend with another friend, whether on purpose or not? What happened? Has anyone gifted you with a mutual friend?

CHAPTER 25

My Personal Friendship with Jesus

All my life I have been a devout Roman Catholic. I love to worship in my Church and receive the Eucharist, which strengthens the life and holiness of Jesus in me. However, as I look back on my life, I realize that in many ways, I have loved Jesus with all my heart, soul, and strength, but I have not loved him with my mind.

It is impossible to love Jesus with your mind until you begin to know him. To try and love what is divine is to wrestle with a mystery beyond ourselves. But to love Jesus in all his humanity is to engage in a "flesh and blood" relationship. It is intimate and real and very human.

As I wrote previously, I have always had a belief in God; through his grace, I have never had a time of doubt. From my earliest memory, I knew that Jesus Christ was my Lord and Savior. However, as a boy, I never studied Scripture systematically.

When I was in high school at University of Detroit Jesuit, we did study Scripture, but it was never presented in the context of a specific plan for our lives. Consequently, I never really identified with the humanity of Jesus.

As Bishop Robert Barron reflects,

> Christ is not simply a human being, and he is not simply God; rather, he is the God-man, the one in whose person divinity and humanity meet. Therefore, it is impossible to love him as God without loving the humanity that he has embraced.[8]

After I made the decision to commit everything in my life to following Jesus, I started to study Scripture. And as I mentioned earlier, when I met Doug Coe, he told me that he would teach me everything he knew about Jesus, provided I made a commitment to pray and read the Gospels every day. Even though I continued to study all of Scripture, Doug's personal commitment to discipling me and sharing Jesus' love was revolutionary in my life.

I would meet Doug in Washington, or if he knew I was traveling on business, he would fly to the airport of the city I was visiting. Before 9/11 the airport clubs were open, and we would meet for two or three hours to study the life of Jesus. Those meetings were precious to me because I drew nearer to the person of Jesus as I learned more about him. Nothing has changed my life more than learning the words and actions of Jesus.

Jesus says that he is "the way and the truth and the life" (John 14:6). In him we discover the purpose of life, and that life becomes an ongoing journey toward him. To follow him, I must know his life, and that means daily reading of and knowing the Gospels. It is in the Gospels that I have learned the supreme knowledge of Jesus and how to imitate him, how to follow in his footsteps.

To live fruitfully as a friend of Jesus, I must identify with him. My daily life must reflect him, and with his grace, I must reproduce him within me. This is why Paul writes about his life in friendship with Jesus, "Yet I live, no longer I, but Christ lives in me" (Galatians 2:20).

It is not enough for me to have a general idea of the Spirit of Jesus. I must know the details of his life—the ways he talked, thought, and acted. I must truly live in him. As a Catholic, I abide in him through Scripture, prayer, and the sacraments. Thus I come to know him more deeply (see Philippians 2 and the First Letter of John). To study the Gospels fruitfully, I must have faith that the teachings of Jesus are contained within them, without error.

The truth is, we only love what we know well. When we love someone, we have a desire to know them on deeper and deeper levels. This is the virtuous cycle of love. I need to know the life of Jesus in my heart and mind so that his words and actions come to my mind in all the different circumstances of my life. In this way, his life penetrates more deeply into mine, and we grow in union.

This is more than just a matter of thinking about Jesus. I must live as the first Twelve did, surrendering myself. I must not hold back but allow the words and life of Jesus to enter deep into my soul and change me.

Believe It or Not

If I want to bring those I love to the Lord, I must first go to the Gospels and study the life of Jesus. Then I can explain to others my friendship with him. Jesus continues to speak to us today; his words are divine and eternal. They are always relevant and up-to-date—especially in our own life. If we cooperate with God's work within us, he will transform us on the inward journey. Then we can be agents of his transformation as we focus outward, on those who don't know him well.

Cardinal Raniero Cantalamessa, the preacher to the papal household, teaches us that, "In the Gospel of John, the personal nature of the act of faith is stressed by the very use of the verb 'to believe.' In the Gospel, we encounter the expression "to believe," which means to lend credence to or hold to be true. . . . We also encounter the expression 'to believe that,' meaning to be convinced that, or just to believe. For instance, to believe that Jesus is the Holy One of God, that he is the Christ, that the Father has sent him."[9]

However, John specifically uses the expression "believe in": "Do not let your hearts be troubled. You have faith in God; have faith also in me" (14:1). *Believing in* the Son of God is different from *believing that* Jesus is the Son of God. If I continue, through God's grace and my ongoing intentional surrender, to believe in Jesus more, my faith in him will eventually become the whole reason for my existence.

As my friendship with Jesus has increased daily, I have been given a faith, hope, and love that have totally changed every aspect of my life. As my friendship with and love for Jesus have grown, I have become the type of husband, father, and friend that God wants me to be. I describe myself now as a New Testament Christian who loves the Lord with all my heart, soul, strength, and mind.

Spending Time with Jesus

Friendship with Jesus shares some qualities with any loving relationship we are in. It isn't simply one decision to surrender, and then we are finished. We must spend ongoing quality time with our beloved. This takes intentionality, time, and effort.

After I committed myself to complete friendship with Jesus, I made a promise to him that if I ever missed a day without talking to him, I would stop doing any ministry that I was involved in. I have kept that promise for over thirty-eight years. Part of that promise is embracing a disciplined life of prayer. By that I mean praying or having a quiet time in the morning and throughout the day. For example, right after I wake up, I begin a time of prayer and then go to daily Mass.

When I was young, a good part of my prayer life consisted of memorized prayers. While heartfelt, they were basically a monologue, with me talking to God but not necessarily listening for any answers. Over the years, as my friendship with Jesus has grown, my prayer life has evolved.

We Catholics have a treasure trove of formal prayers that are, in essence, a form of poetry that we address in a loving way to God. One of my favorites is the *Anima Christi;* this prayer always leads me into a deeper discussion with Jesus:

Soul of Christ, sanctify me.
Body of Christ, save me.
Blood of Christ, inebriate me.
Water from the side of Christ, wash me.
Passion of Christ, strengthen me.
O Good Jesus, hear me.
Within your wounds hide me.
Permit me not to be separated from you.
From the wicked foe, defend me.
At the hour of my death, call me
and bid me come to you
That with your saints I may praise you
For ever and ever. Amen.

Another powerful way I spend time with Jesus is through the Rosary. I have prayed the Rosary daily for over thirty-six years. It is a beautiful way of immersing oneself in the love of Jesus.

Many people do not understand the Rosary. Originally it was designed so that men and women unable to read or not fully conversant with Scripture could meditate on the life of Jesus as they prayed through the mysteries of the Rosary. These mysteries revolve around the life, ministry, death, and resurrection of Jesus, as well as key moments in the life of his mother, Mary, whose whole life points toward Jesus. For me, praying the Rosary is like hearing beautiful music; it brings my heart into union with Jesus as I ponder his life and teachings.

My daily prayer life is really a dialogue with Jesus, in which I talk to him about everything. This did not just happen the moment I experienced my conversion. In many ways, prayer is like running a marathon. It takes intentionality to embrace the discipline of prayer. Every day that you pray, you are, through God's grace, strengthening your spiritual muscles so that you can pray longer and more deeply.

When I first began to pray, my spiritual muscles were not very developed. By embracing the discipline of prayer, I actively cooperated with God's grace. He continues to lead me more deeply into the practice of prayer.

There were some seminal moments in which Jesus revealed to me how he wanted me to talk to him on an ongoing basis, throughout my day. One occurred in 1989, when I was walking with Mother Teresa through the slums of Calcutta, and we were discussing prayer. Earlier that day, she had told me that she prayed two hours in the morning and two hours at night. She quickly pointed out that she was not married, did not have children, and had a freedom that I did not have. Therefore she had the ability to pray more than most people.

But as we were walking, Mother Teresa said, "I told you how I pray, but that's not really accurate." She explained, "I feel like I'm praying all the time. Look at what we are talking about today? We are talking about Jesus, and that is a prayer."

I have thought extensively about what it means to pray all the time, and I have made it a goal. Throughout the day I am reminded of Jesus in small ways. You could call these reminders "microbursts of prayer." They happen in response to what's going on in my life. A constant prayer life is essential to deepening our friendship with Jesus.

Contemplative Prayer

As I recounted in my other book, I had great difficulty in entering into contemplative prayer until one day, miraculously, God gave me a word that unlocked my mind and allowed me to go deeper. That word was "yield." This happened after daily Mass; I stayed to pray after the liturgy was concluded.

At that time, I always ended my prayers with "Lord, I love you with all my heart, soul, mind, and strength. Help me to love my neighbor for my love of you." On this day I heard a voice in my mind, saying, "That is not true. You are too imperfect. Why don't you pray it this way? Yield your heart to my heart, so that you have peace of heart. Yield your soul to my soul, so that you are one with me, the Father, and Holy Spirit. Why don't you yield your mind to my mind, so that you think, talk, and act like me? Why don't you yield your strength to my strength, so that you have strength for everything that I want you to do?"

That is now how I conclude my morning prayer.

I also have a special time in the late afternoon, as well as another before I go to bed, when I have some concentrated prayer time with Jesus. Finally, every night before we go to sleep, Nancy and I pray. We commit ourselves to the care of Jesus and petition for our family and friends, as detailed in chapter 14.

I know that Jesus is omnipresent—that he has been, is, and always will be with me. However, I have come to understand that there is a difference between recognizing that Jesus is *with me* and recognizing that Jesus is *in me*. In John's Gospel, John the Baptist makes this profound statement: "He must increase; I must decrease" (3:30).

The more I understand that Jesus is in me, the more I understand that I must decrease. My will and desires must be surrendered to him. Jesus in turn can use the intimate friendship he has given me to reach others. All the ways I have discussed here to spend time with Jesus transform me further, so that I can think, talk, and act like Jesus, with greater impact and fruitfulness.

Personal Application

Take a few moments, either by yourself or in a small group, and reflect on the following questions. You can share your answers with others when you have finished your reflection.

1. In this chapter, the author makes a distinction between believing that Jesus is the Son of God and believing in Jesus. How would you explain that distinction to someone who might ask you to do so?

2. What are some of the ways that you spend time with Jesus? Do you find yourself with space in your life to do these things regularly and intentionally? Why or why not?

3. What role does Jesus play in your life? If someone asked you to describe how your life is different because you encountered Jesus, what would you say?

CHAPTER 26

The Need for Friendship in the Christian Church

Every major Christian denomination is experiencing a rapid year-over-year decline in numbers. According to a Pew Research Center report from October 2019, the largest "religious" subgroup in American society is "nones," those who profess no religious affiliation. Nones have increased to 26 percent, while Catholics have slipped from 23 percent in 2009 to 20 percent in 2019.[10] COVID has accelerated the decline in church affiliation.

While mainline denominations have declined rapidly over the last forty years, it is likely that the rise in young nones will lead to a "demographic cliff" in the major churches. This concern hits the Catholic Church as well. The latest Gallup Poll states that fewer than four in ten Catholics attend church in any given week.[11] Catholic attendance is down 6 percent over the past decade. The only reason the Catholic population in the US has remained relatively stable is due to the huge influx of the Hispanic population. As Gallup points out, troubling signs for both Protestants and Catholics are that younger adults, particularly those aged twenty-one to twenty-nine, are less likely to identify themselves as either Protestant or Catholic.

The declining trends in attendance will have tremendous financial repercussions. Catholics and mainline denominations will be unable to afford the number of churches, schools, and other social programs they presently operate.

Two key indicators of vitality in the Catholic Church—Baptisms and marriages—have declined dramatically throughout the United States over the past fifty years. Baptisms have declined by more than 50 percent, and the number of marriages is at its lowest since 1965. Baptisms and marriages are indicators for the future: Baptism represents the sacrament of initiation into a Christ-centered life, and marriage represents the beginning of what we call the domestic Church. Of the marriages in the Church, one out of every four ends in divorce.[12] In addition, the Sacrament of Confirmation is often considered by the young as the last thing they have to do before they stop going to Mass.

According to another Pew survey, six people leave the Catholic Church for every one convert who enters each year. In my opinion, one of the main reasons is the failure of the Church in America to highlight the humanity of Jesus and his teachings in the Gospels and to focus on bringing people into friendship with him. The truth is that Jesus has chosen each of us to be his friend. He pointed out the sacrificial nature of this authentic friendship in the Gospel of John:

> This is my commandment: love one another as I love you. No one has greater love than this, to lay down one's life for one's friends. You are my friends if you do what I command you. I no longer call you slaves, because a slave does not know what his master is doing. I have called you friends, because I have told you everything I have heard from my Father. (15:12-15)

Friendship, Jesus tells us, is a deep and essential act of love for someone. He said that those who love are willing to lay down their lives for one another. Jesus knew that the Twelve, as well as all of his disciples, would have to endure sacrifice and suffering as they followed him on "the Way" (Acts 9:2).

The beloved disciple tells us that "God is love" (1 John 4:8). Jesus invites us into friendship because he desires an intimate union of love with us. He reveals everything he has heard from his Father and pours out on us his love and life through the power of the Holy Spirit so that our hearts might be conformed to his. All of this begins in Jesus, who has chosen us to be his disciples.

We respond to this invitation and dedicate our lives to Jesus Christ, our Lord, as we bear his name in the world. The work of the Church begins in the friendship of Jesus, who enables us to go and bear fruit. "I . . . chose you and appointed you to go and bear fruit that will remain" (John 15:16).

Part of the failure to invite people into friendship with Jesus has to do with what Bishop Robert Barron calls "Beige Christianity":

When I recall my Catholic youth in the late sixties and seventies, I think of the color beige. It seemed to be an overriding concern of [those] who formed my generation to make our Catholicism as non-threatening, accessible, culturally appealing, as possible. . . . Doctrinal peculiarities were set aside in favor of generally humanistic ethical values; liturgies were designed to be, above all, entertaining; . . . There was, above all, a hand-wringing and apologetic quality to the Catholicism of my youth.[13]

We see this in the Catholic Church quite clearly. It is a rarity for any Catholic to hear a homily on the Real Presence of Jesus in the Eucharist. Marriage is discussed in passing, and the reality of Jesus as both God and man has not been conveyed to the general population. Catholics who are faithful to the Church love the traditional ritual and beauty of the Mass, but unfortunately, that is often detached from the humanity of Jesus. If you begin to talk about friendship with Jesus, you receive a blank stare, because many Catholics have never considered that a possibility.

Another Pew survey in 2019 showed that 69 percent of Catholics do not believe that the bread and wine at Mass become the Body and Blood of Christ. Rather, they believe that the bread and wine are mere symbols of the body and blood of Jesus Christ. The Pew report also stated that most Catholics who believe bread and wine are only symbolic do not know the Church's teaching on transubstantiation. In addition, forty-three percent of Catholics believe that the Church actually teaches that the bread and wine are symbolic.[14]

Bishop Robert Barron posted on Twitter on August 6, 2019: "It is hard to describe how angry I feel after reading what the latest Pew Research study reveals about understanding of the Eucharist amongst Catholics. This should be a wake-up call to all of us in the Church." He went on to say, "It has been a massive failure of the Church carrying on its own tradition."[15]

As I have said, the root of all this is that Christians simply do not know who Jesus is or the reason for his Incarnation, life, death, and resurrection. The theme of this book is friendship with Jesus and friendship with others because of Jesus. I have attempted to point out the different friendships that have affected major decisions in my life. The inspiration for the book, however, was the apparent absence of fruit from our evangelization efforts as a universal Church, demonstrated by the decreased morality and increased secularization of our society.

I believe that we don't bear much fruit in evangelization because we have failed to evangelize in the way the apostles and their disciples evangelized in the early Church. They talked about Jesus as a friend, both human and divine, and they explained that Jesus had come to start a family of men and women who would do the will of his Father. Although many Catholic parishes foster Bible study, pastors need to urge all parishioners to study the Gospels. If this Christian decline is going to be reversed, it will only be through the teachings of Jesus and the realization that God was in Christ to reconcile us to the Father *as his friends*.

I have a unique perspective to advance such thoughts. I am a lifelong Roman Catholic who has served on numerous

Evangelical boards, such as Leighton Ford Ministries, Promise Keepers, the Navigators, Prison Fellowship International, Prison Fellowship Ministries, Alpha International, and the New Canaan Society. I have also chaired Prison Fellowship International for sixteen years, succeeding Chuck Colson, as well as succeeding him at Prison Fellowship Ministries and serving as its chairman for five years. During most of the time I was serving on such boards, I was also president of the Archdiocese of Detroit Endowment Foundation Board, as well as one of the founders of the National Fellowship of Catholic Men.

In traveling to over 120 countries, I have seen the power of proclaiming the person of Jesus in prisons on every continent, as well as to leaders of nations, including most of the Muslim nations. My goal for this book is to lead people to Jesus. I use quotations from Scripture, not as a formula to get people to accept him, but to present Jesus as the living God who desires our friendship—no matter who we are or where we currently find ourselves or what we have done.

I have learned that true evangelization is a personal, interior journey. By coming closer to Jesus as a friend, we are better able to love others and to share with them who Jesus really is. By recounting numerous instances from around the world where I have represented Jesus, I hope the reader will be inspired to do the same.

I hope to help evangelizers understand how critical it is to use words when evangelizing—not just any words, but specifically the words of Jesus. Using a methodology other than the words of Jesus simply does not work. Secondly, most Catholics (and non-Catholics) never hear anything about Jesus from a committed Catholic layman or laywoman. I want that to change. Lastly, I want to help the average man and woman accept the reality of being friends with Jesus.

This is my hope and also my prayer for you.

In Jesus' name.

Amen.

Author's Note

In addition to the friends that I mentioned throughout this book, there are many other men who have demonstrated Jesus to me and my family. It would be impossible to recount the differences these men have made in my life, men such as Tony Cimmarrusti, Jim Towey, Gil Cox, Dan Megler, Tom Cunnington, Tom Cole, Jack Krasula, and my NCS brothers, to name only a few.

Notes

1. Ralph Martin, *A Church in Crisis: Pathways Forward* (Steubenville, OH: Emmaus Road Publishing, 2020), 88, quoting the International Theological Commission, "Some Current Questions in Eschatology," 10.3, 1992, vatican.va/roman_curia/congregations/cfaith/cti_documents/rc_cti_1990_problemi-attuali-escatologia_en.html.

2. Belinda Luscombe, "Why 25% of Millennials Will Never Get Married," *Time*, September 24, 2014, https://time.com/3422624/report-millennials-marriage/.

3. New Canaan Society, newcanaansociety.org/about/mission/.

4. New Canaan Society, newcanaansociety.org/about/.

5. Nicky Gumbel, "Three Keys to Great Friendships," Bible in One Year, Day 174, bibleinoneyear.org/en/classic/174/.

6. Josemaría Escrivá, *The Way*, no. 303 (Manila, Philippines: Scriptor, 1982), 83.

7. C. S. Lewis, *The Four Loves*, chap. 4, in *The Beloved Works of C. S. Lewis* (New York: Inspirational Press), 244.

8. Bishop Robert Barron, Gospel Reflection, March 20, 2020, as quoted by Mats Tunehag, "Most Read 2020: The Coronavirus Pandemic and BAM: Seven Things We Can Do," *Business as Mission,* December 10, 2020, businessasmission.com/the-coronavirus-pandemic-and -bam-seven-things-we-can-do-most-read/.

9. Cardinal Raniero Cantalamessa, *Jesus Christ: The Holy One of God,* trans. Alan Neame (Collegeville, MN: Liturgical Press, 1991), 63.

10. Pew Research Center, "In U.S., Decline of Christianity Continues at Rapid Pace," October 17, 2019, pewresearch.org/religion/2019/10/17/ in-u-s-decline-of-christianity-continues-at-rapid-pace/.

11. Lydia Saad, "Catholics' Church Attendance Resumes Downward Slide," Gallup, April 9, 2018, https://news. gallup.com/poll/232226/church-attendance-among-catholics-resumes-downward-slide.aspx.

12. Michael Lipka, "Most U.S. Catholics Hope for Change in Church Rule on Divorce, Communion," Pew Research Center, October 26, 2015, https:// www.pewresearch.org/fact-tank/2015/10/26/ most-u-s-catholics-hope-for-change-in-church-rule-on-divorce-communion/.

13. Bishop Robert Barron, *Bridging the Great Divide: Musings of a Post-liberal, Post-conservative, Evangelical Catholic* (Lanham, MD: Rowman & Littlefield Publishers, Inc., 2004), 17.

14. Pew Research Center, "Just One-Third of U.S. Catholics Agree with Their Church That Eucharist Is Body, Blood of Christ," August 5, 2019, https://www.pewresearch.org/fact-tank/2019/08/05/transubstantiation-eucharist-u-s-catholics/.

15. Bishop Robert Barron (@BishopBarron), "It's hard to describe how angry I feel," Twitter, August 6, 2019, 5:37 p.m., https://twitter.com/BishopBarron/status/1158854745316057090?ref_src=twsrc%5Etfw.

About the Author

Mike Timmis was born in Detroit, Michigan, where he has had a distinguished career as both an attorney and a businessman. He earned his undergraduate degree from Wayne State University and graduated with highest honors from the Wayne State Law School in 1965. He was an editor of *Law Review* while in law school. He received the school's Distinguished Law Alumni Award in 1979.

In 1991, Governor John Engler appointed Mr. Timmis as a governor of Wayne State University, the term of which expired December 31, 1996. In 1993, Mr. Timmis was the recipient of the Business and Professional Award from Religious Heritage of America. In the year 2000, Mr. Timmis was named Entrepreneur of the Year by Students in Free Enterprise. Further, Mr. Timmis received an honorary doctorate in humane letters from the University of Detroit-Mercy in May of 1995, in recognition of his civic and humanitarian contributions. In May 2008, Mr. Timmis received a doctorate from Ave Maria University.

Mr. Timmis was senior partner of the law firm of Timmis & Inman, LLP. He was also the cofounder and vice chairman of Talon LLC., a privately owned company formed in 1973 with extensive interests in retail and manufacturing, both in the United States and Europe, as well as real estate. Mr. Timmis retired on December 31, 2007.

In addition to his legal and business involvements, Mr. Timmis holds memberships in many professional associations, is a director of numerous corporations, and has served on the boards of many charitable organizations and foundations, including St. John Healthcare Systems and Cornerstone schools. Mr. Timmis has served on many ministry boards, including The Navigators, Promise Keepers, and Prison Fellowship Ministries. He served for sixteen years as chairman of Prison Fellowship International, a transdenominational Christian organization with 129 chartered countries. In October 2006, Mr. Timmis succeeded Chuck Colson as chairman of Prison Fellowship Ministries (USA), which he chaired until June of 2011.

Currently, Mr. Timmis is on the board of Alpha International and Alpha in Prisons, both of which are based in London, England, as well as the Advisory Board of Alpha in a Catholic Context. He is also on the board of the New Canaan Society.

Mr. Timmis and his wife, Nancy, are deeply involved in the problems of the poor and have developed self-help projects in Africa and Central and South America. They are also very active in addressing the educational needs of children in East Africa as well as in the city of Detroit. Along with his partner, Mr. Randolph Agley, Mr. Timmis was named one of the "Leaders of the Nineties" by *Crain's Detroit Business* magazine.

Mr. Timmis has been married to the former Nancy Lauppe for sixty years. The Timmises have two children, Michael and Laura. Laura died thirty-six years ago. Michael and his wife (also named Laura) lived in Uganda for seven years, lifting up Christ to the poor through various projects. This work continues in seven schools, multiple homes, and various programs for street children and the rural poor and has expanded from Uganda to Rwanda, Tanzania, and South Sudan. Today approximately two thousand young people are in various Christ-centered programs.

Michael Timmis, Jr., is past chairman of Ave Maria University and current president of the Timmis Family Foundation. He and his wife earned MBAs from the University of Michigan School of Business. They now live in Florida and have four daughters and one son. The senior Timmises are residents of Naples, Florida, and return to Grosse Pointe Farms, Michigan, during the summer.

Mike Timmis' autobiography was published in February 2008 by NavPress. It is entitled *Between Two Worlds: The Spiritual Journey of an Evangelical Catholic*.

the WORD
among us®
The *Spirit* of Catholic Living

This book was published by The Word Among Us. Since 1981, The Word Among Us has been answering the call of the Second Vatican Council to help Catholic laypeople encounter Christ in the Scriptures.

The name of our company comes from the prologue to the Gospel of John and reflects the vision and purpose of all of our publications: to be an instrument of the Spirit, whose desire is to manifest Jesus' presence in and to the children of God. In this way, we hope to contribute to the Church's ongoing mission of proclaiming the gospel to the world so that all people would know the love and mercy of our Lord and grow more deeply in their faith as missionary disciples.

Our monthly devotional magazine, *The Word Among Us*, features meditations on the daily and Sunday Mass readings, and currently reaches more than one million Catholics in North America and another half million Catholics in one hundred countries around the world. Our book division, The Word Among Us Press, publishes numerous books, Bible studies, and pamphlets that help Catholics grow in their faith.

To learn more about who we are and what we publish, log on to our website at www.wau.org. There you will find a variety of Catholic resources that will help you grow in your faith.

Embrace His Word, Listen to God . . .

www.wau.org